Culture, Architecture, and Design

Culture, Architecture, and Design

Amos Rapoport

Architectural and Planning Research Book Series
Andrew D. Seidel, Series Editor

Locke Science Publishing Company, Inc.

Contents

Figures

INTRODUCTION

The underlying premise of this book is that architecture is *not* a 'free' artistic activity but a science-based profession that is concerned with problem solving. Moreover, these problems need to be *discovered* and *identified*, not 'defined' by designers, i.e., not invented. It follows, therefore, that architecture and related design fields, such as urban design, landscape architecture, interior design, and, up to a point, even product design together comprise the field of *environmental design*. This is the term I will use throughout.

The purpose of environmental design is not for its practitioners to express themselves 'artistically.' An 'extreme' formulation of the consequences of this position is that designers' satisfaction should come from problem identification and solving. Designers might thus need to produce environments that they themselves may detest if they work for the users concerned. The purpose of design is then to create environments and their constituent parts that suit users, i.e., settings and their 'furnishings' that are supportive for these users, their wants, activities, and so on. I thus take design to be user oriented, designers being surrogates for users. This means that the products of such design (buildings and other physical environments) must be based on an understanding of human characteristics and must fit and be supportive of those. This will be elaborated later, but in the case of this book, designs need to respond to 'culture,' i.e., be culture-specific.

Knowledge and design

It then follows that design must be based on knowledge of how people and environments interact, i.e., on research (basic and applied) on environment-behavior relations (EBR); design becomes the application of research-based knowledge. Such knowledge need not, nor can it ever be, perfect (it will change with advances in research), but it must be based on the best available knowledge at any given time, i.e., to be at 'the state of the art.' This means knowing and keeping up with the literature, so that design can be based on up-to-date research, not on designers' personal preferences, intuition, and the like; although sometimes intuition can lead to hypotheses (and is essential in

1

research and science generally), which need to be tested rather than accepted on the basis of wishful thinking.

Such research is needed not only in design but in the full sequence of essential activities, those that should precede it, such as problem analysis and programming (*what* should be designed and *why*), and lead to hypotheses, which can then be researched, and those which should follow design — post-occupancy evaluation. This is important if the design fields are to learn both from failures and successes rather than repeat mistakes and not know why success has occurred. In order to know what success is, two things are necessary: first, what the design needs to do to solve the problem(s) so that one can judge if it does — post occupancy evaluation (not "architectural criticism," which merely represents the personal preferences of the critic and is thus of no interest or value). This is essential because any design can be seen as an hypothesis of the form: If so and so is done, such and such will happen. This must then be tested. Only in this way will one be able to repeat successes reliably and predictably. Only in this way can design itself become a form of research, which, at the moment, it cannot be despite occasional claims to the contrary.

Second, in order even to know what success is, two things are essential: first, knowing clearly what the design needs to do in order to solve the problem(s), because only then can one judge whether it does it well, badly, or at all. This means that goals and objectives need to be explicitly stated and their validity justified by reference to knowledge of EBR. Second, if design is meant to create 'better' environments, one needs to know: What is better? Better for whom? Why is it better? How does one know that it is better? And so on.

I will illustrate this last point through three 'extreme' examples. These are cases in which issues can be seen particularly clearly, in black and white as it were, rather than in the more common "shades of gray." These 'extreme' examples are typically developing countries, groups undergoing rapid and extreme culture change, and their tribal and vernacular environments. These can serve as 'model systems,' analogous to those used, as one example, in biomedical research. Such situations, although not only those, will be used throughout this book.

The first example concerns the introduction of piped, or running, water into North African villages by French architects. The result, at the time, was dissatisfaction and resistance by the residents. Investigation showed that for women in *purdah* (i.e., kept rather strictly isolated), visits to village wells were an important social occasion (what I will later call 'latent function,' in this case of getting water). The provision of taps eliminated that important social and information exchange occasion. The women were unhappy and complained to the men, who then took action.

The second example concerns a group of Motilone Indians in the Amazon forest on the Colombia-Venezuela border. Their dwelling and settlement are one and the same — a large communal dwelling holding from 10 to 30 households called a *bohio* (communal dwellings are common in Amazonia and found elsewhere). The *bohio* is a circular structure built of thatch, which almost reaches the ground so that the dwelling is in semi-darkness. Each family has a space on the periphery defined by partitions where hammocks are hung. Each family also has a fire on the earth floor in front of its space so that all the cooking fires face the large central public space, effectively blocking the view into the family areas. Thus, in the afternoon one might see a father back from hunting, gently swinging in his hammock, playing with a child in the privacy provided by the woman cooking a meal on the fire.

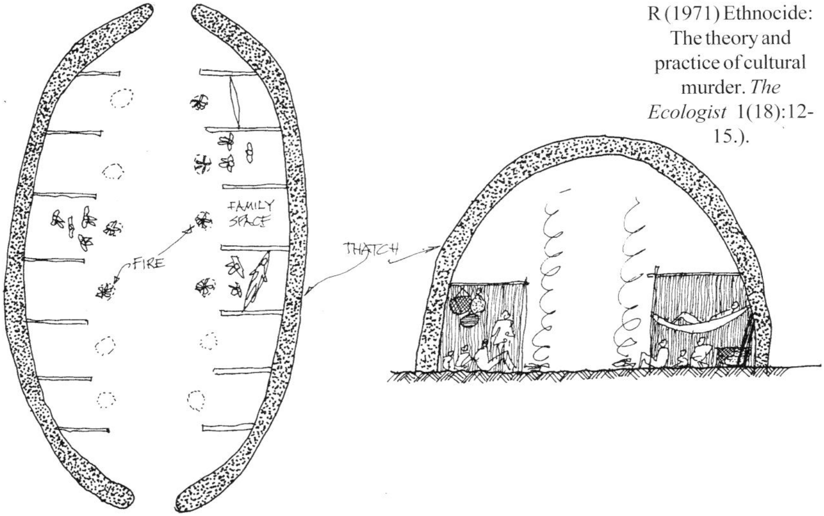

FIGURE 1A. Motilone *bohio* (based on verbal description in Jaulin R (1971) Ethnocide: The theory and practice of cultural murder. *The Ecologist* 1(18):12-15.).

3

Introduction

Well-meaning people, feeling that this was a barbaric way to live — on an earth floor in perpetual twilight with open fires and smoke — substituted light, open, airy and breezy, metal-roofed sheds with concrete floors and electric lighting. This should clearly have been an improvement but, as will be seen shortly, that was not the case.

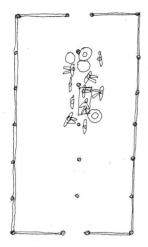

FIGURE 1B. Motilone replacement housing (based on verbal description in Jaulin, *op.cit.*).

The third example concerns an Australian aboriginal traditional camp. Each family has its space, defined by sweeping the ground several times a day, which contains a small windbreak (a *wiltja*). The fires are at the edge of the family space nearest the large central public space. At night, the fires in the darkness of the bush prevent people seeing each other across the central space (very much as in the case of the Motilone Indian). At the same time there is a great deal of acoustic interaction.

In this case also, well-meaning people, apparently feeling that this was much too primitive, built houses arranged along streets. When, due to their unsuitability for their lifestyle, the Aborigines refused to live in them and recreated the camp form, these well-meaning people improved the situation by providing electric lighting in the camp — after all, the bush is *very* dark at night. But again, as we shall see shortly, that was not an improvement.

'Improvements' and their consequences

In each of these cases, the 'improvement,' in fact, had major negative consequences because of the complex relationships among culture, behavior, and the built environ-

4

ment, which this book discusses, and which greatly affect the notion of 'good' or 'better' environments. This is because even minor changes in a complex system like that relating particular cultures, their social mechanisms, lifestyles and activity systems, and built environments, may have major and unforeseen consequences (without research-based knowledge) elsewhere in the system — a truth already known about (other) ecological systems. Thus, apparently benign, well-meaning 'improvements' may sometimes be more dangerous to a group than apparently much more malignant, destructive changes.

An interesting example of the latter is provided by the case of the Australian aboriginal group of the Yir-Yiront (West coast of Cape York) for whom a devastating encounter with some white cattlemen, who killed or wounded most of them, proved easily forgotten — 70 years later the group had recovered and there was no memory of this event. On the other hand, the introduction of steel axes, an apparently benign, non-coercive change, led to major social disorganization since the production and use of stone axes was a central element in the culture: it set up rights and obligations between the sexes, affected the prestige of older men, maintained political and economic links with distant tribes, and related to traditions and origin myths. All activities — routine and ceremonial — were linked to the stone axes. The sudden introduction of steel axes, which gave no time for adaptation, proved destructive. It thus follows that drastic change that is too rapid can be destructive, i.e., when the extent of change is too large, when it happens too quickly, when it is not desired, and when the people concerned feel that they have no control over the changes that are happening. Under these conditions the results of change can be critical. What generally works much better is slower change, allowing for what we might call *creative adaptation* — the rejection of some innovations, the adoption of others, and their integration into the cultural system. In the present context, the important consequence is that environmental quality or the classification of environments as 'better' or 'worse' is not absolute or self-evident but relative and a matter of definition, i.e., it is based on judgments relative to certain cultural values and norms.

Using a distinction from anthropology, it is necessary to consider concepts such as environmental quality *emically*, **Emics vs. etics**

Introduction

from inside the culture as it were, emphasizing what members of that group themselves emphasize, rather than *etically*, from the perspective of an outside observer. Researchers and designers are typically outsiders; they have to use etics. Therefore, in practice both etics and emics are needed. The major point is that emics need to be understood before developing etic aspects (e.g., comparative, 'neutral,' cross-culturally valid concepts and principles).

Reasons for negative consequences

Why did the three 'improvements' described have negative consequences? In the case of the North African village, the problem had to do with social interaction and communication, the latent function of fetching water. In the case of a society where women are in *purdah*, the periodic visits to the village well provide one of the few (if not only) occasions to leave the house, gossip, interact, and relate to the communication network — obtaining and passing on information. All these critical activities and mechanisms are disrupted by the simple act of introducing running water into each dwelling.

In the case of the Motilone Indian *bohio*, the thatched dwelling was not only relatively cool but also mosquito proof (as well as proof against much of the over-abundant minor wildlife of the area). In the family areas, women could spin and weave, rest, and look after the children. When together, the family had privacy due to the shape of the *bohio* and the fires on the public side. The rectangular modern dwellings were designed to admit the maximum amount of light on the principle that light is good while darkness is evil, and the central cooking area was missing. This seriously disrupted social life and the division of responsibility and destroyed the intimacy of family life. The lack of the perpetual half-light had eliminated the needed restful retreat from the heat, glare, and fierce sunlight of the area. This half-light also provided a major mechanism of achieving privacy and intimacy, a process helped by the location of the fires, which blocked the view into the family areas. With neither relaxation nor intimacy possible, social and family relations are badly disrupted.

While the thick thatch and darkness of the *bohio* discourage insects, the electric light and openness of the new dwellings attract wildlife. The result is a deterioration in physical well-being. The elimination of solid walls so as to achieve cross-ventilation has another effect: the heavy rains of the area force people away from the open periphery into the center with an increase in crowding and further erosion of privacy and intimacy. The lack of individual cooking adjacent to the family area has destroyed the intimacy of the family meal.

The substitution of a concrete floor for the earth floor provides a particularly striking example of the unforeseen consequences that follow changes that fail to consider cultural patterns. For example, the Motilone looms' need to be driven into the floor was made impossible by concrete. Weaving became impossible, and tattered modern garments replaced traditional clothing. This has led to a loss of self-respect and also a deterioration in physical health. Also, children urinate and defecate on the floors (nappies, even if one could afford them, are culturally inappropriate, hot and sweaty, and make children much dirtier). Earth floors are extremely easily cleaned — concrete floors are impossible to keep clean: they soon become appallingly dirty. In fact, the introduction of all sorts of modern, 'improved' elements has generally made life dirtier, less healthy, and more sordid.

Specific examples in this one case could be continued, but generally each detail that was changed — the clothing, dwelling, cooking utensils, organization of time, activities, and social relations — have all contributed to the destruction of the culture.

In the case of the Australian aborigines, I wish to discuss just one mechanism affected by the introduction of electric light: the destruction of privacy and of a very culture-specific, conflict-resolving mechanism — although the camp, in its spatial organization, has many other important and significant relationships to social structure and interaction, ritual, relationship to the land, and so on.

In the evening, each family in the camp sits in its own space around the private side of the fire. This is the time for ritualized grieving — mourning the departed by 'wailing.' This creates a particular auditory environment, elicits a form of communal empathy, and helps contribute to the 'welding' of the individuals into a tightly knit, supportive social unit. (This is, of course, reinforced by a large number of other devices, some of which depend on the camp organization.) The darkness and the spatial organization of the camp also enable a very important, and a highly culture-specific, form of conflict resolution to take place, allowing both communal issues and personal grievances to be aired and settled. In the case of a personal dispute, the proponent will loudly proclaim his grievance. This may last for several hours and be repeated over several evenings. Communal issues are aired in a similar way. In both cases, everyone may follow the argument, although not everyone may wish to participate. Consensual agreement is eventually reached, as it must be because it is *always* consensus rather than majority rule which operates.

In this process, both the spatial organization of the camp and, even more importantly, the level of illumination play an important role. In fact, the amicable resolution of conflict might be said to depend on the latter. Only at dusk or later when visual displays are impossible does a person give expression to his emotions. It is possible that this is a ritualized way of separating visual and aural aggressive displays, thus avoiding and preventing physical conflict by keeping the level of conflict low: the additive effect of more than one sensory channel carrying information (i.e., the redundancy) is reduced. Note that the darkness is reinforced by the location of the fires on the space side of the family groups, which further isolates people from each other visually; it is almost impossible to see past the blazing fires,

FIGURE 2. Diagrammatic layout of aboriginal camp (based on personal communication from P Hamilton, 1972.).

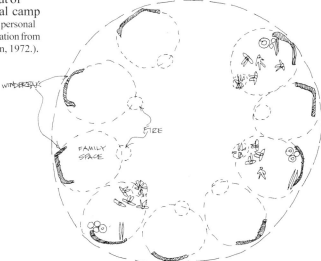

WINDBREAK

FIRE

FAMILY SPACE

as is the case in the Motilone *bohio*. The physical separation of people is also reinforced by the spatial organization of the camp with its relatively large central space, which makes visual contact more difficult, and also by the custom that *after dark* people do not leave their *wiltja* and the area around it. This is due to the belief that malignant spirits (*mamu*) are about.

Thus, a number of mechanisms assure that only the auditory modality can be used in this process. Even if the spatial organization is kept, the introduction of artificial light disrupts this whole set of conflict-resolving mechanisms: people can see each other since it is no longer dark, they are free to leave their *wiltja*, and so on. The result is a much higher level of physical violence, which also tends to be raised by other changes in the environment and lifestyle, e.g., increasing density and non-availability of mobility to avoid conflict — a mechanism much used by nomads generally.

I am *not* suggesting that running water, concrete floors, daylight, and the absence of smoke and night lighting are undesirable. What I *am* suggesting is that whether they result in 'better' environments depends on lifestyle, rules, social arrangements, stage of acculturation, development of new social mechanisms, values, norms, ideals, and so on. As these change, so will the evaluation of environments and changes to environments, and hence also the acceptability and desirability of environments.

Do 'improvements' result in 'better' environments?

The social, cultural, and physical aspects need to be considered together. Moreover, *a priori* (and arbitrarily) one cannot assume that any given change to the environment, which all design inevitably is, will be an improvement. Environmental quality is always perceived environmental quality and is contextual in terms of how people and environments interact — generally and in any given case. In the three examples discussed, this interaction is mediated by cultural mechanisms. This suggests that in design among the various human variables that need to be considered, cultural variables play a significant role. This is the topic of this book.

CHAPTER 1

The Nature and Role of Environment-Behavior Studies

Research on EBR and this approach are generally the subject matter of the field of environment-behavior studies (EBS), and I will be dealing with the role of culture in design within that framework. But before discussing this, I need to discuss the nature of EBS.

The three basic questions of EBS

The field of EBS is best described by what I call the three basic questions:

(1) What bio-social, psychological, and cultural characteristics of human beings (as members of a species, as individuals, and as members of various groups) influence (and, in design, *should* influence) which characteristics of the built environment?

(2) What effects do which aspects of which environments have on which groups of people, under what circumstances (i.e., in what context) and when, why, and how?

(3) Given this two-way interaction between people and environments, there must be mechanisms that link them. What are these mechanisms?

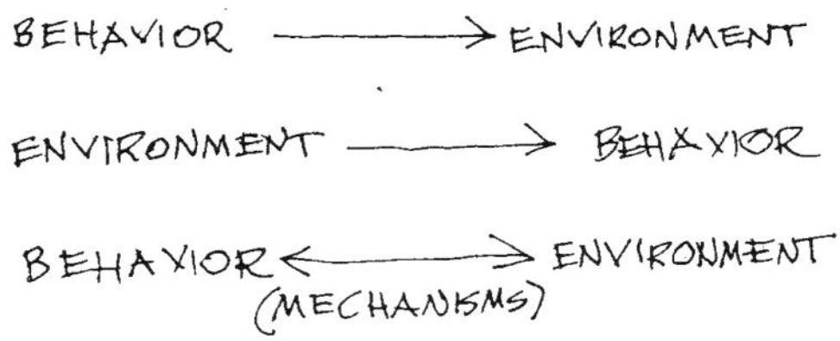

FIGURE 3. The three basic questions of EBS.

BEHAVIOR ⟶ ENVIRONMENT

ENVIRONMENT ⟶ BEHAVIOR

BEHAVIOR ⟵⟶ ENVIRONMENT
(MECHANISMS)

I now discuss each of these questions briefly; various other aspects of them, and their implications, will become clear and will be developed as we discuss the specific topic with which this book is concerned.

Knowledge about humans

The first question concerns all that we already know, are learning, and will learn in the future about human beings.

In other words, our knowledge, as is the case in all science, is not once and for all but open-ended and developing. This knowledge is about all characteristics of human beings because *a priori* one does not know which might be relevant regarding the built environment, even though currently they do not apparently concern design. This knowledge is then about human evolution, biology, psychology, social relations, cultural attributes, and many other aspects. This means that EBS researchers need to keep up with research in a number of fields that deal with human characteristics.

The second question directly affects design. If the effects of the environment on people are important, then design efforts may need to be increased; if they are minimal (as some social scientists believe), then much of the investment of effort and resources by both researchers and designers may be inappropriate. The question is also often put incorrectly. It implies that somehow people are placed in environments that then have an effect on them. In reality, under most conditions, people choose and select environments, and this process of habitat selection (found in all living organisms) is the most important aspect of the effect of environment on people.[1]

Effects of environment and habitat selection

Habitat selection involves both rejecting or leaving undesirable, unsuitable, unsupportive, or inhibiting environments (what are called *pushes*) and seeking out desired, suitable, and supportive environments (what are called *pulls*).

Also, environments are not determining, i.e., they cannot generate behavior (in the broadest sense of people's actions, thoughts, feelings, etc.). They can be either facilitating or inhibiting for certain behaviors, cognitive processes, moods, and so on. It can be suggested that inhibiting environments have a larger effect than facilitating ones. It is easier to block behaviors than to generate them; in fact, the latter is impossible (one can bring a horse to water but not make it drink). Sometimes new behaviors seem to follow environmental changes, but they are best understood as the result of environments acting as 'catalysts' — they release behaviors that had previously been blocked by highly inhibiting environments.

Chapter 1

Criticality In this connection, the idea of *criticality* is very important. Higher criticality refers to situations where environments have more effects on people who in some way have 'reduced competence,' whether due to illness, age, excessively rapid culture change, or other factors. For such people, the additional stress and effort needed to overcome inhibiting effects becomes too demanding. In such cases, highly supportive environments become necessary and the role of various specific elements of the environment in supporting critical social and cultural patterns and mechanisms needs to be discovered and used in planning and design.

Also, the effects of the environment on people can be direct (the attributes and qualities of the environment acting directly on people's activities, moods, and so on) or indirect. In the latter case, environments provide cues that are used to interpret a social situation, and the effects on people follow from the definition of that situation. In this sense, the environment can be seen as a form of non-verbal communication. If the cues are noticed and understood, i.e., made clear enough (e.g., through redundancy), and are culturally appropriate, the social contexts can be judged correctly and behavior adjusted accordingly. This is the critical aspect of *settings* and how they work, to be discussed later in Chapter 2. This also implies the existence of rules, norms, schemata, and the like, and hence the important role of culture in that process. The importance of cultural specificity in the organization of environments (what is called 'design') also follows.

Identifying mechanisms that link people and environments Regarding question three, the importance of identifying mechanisms cannot be over-emphasized. Both in understanding phenomena and in being able predictably to modify them (i.e., 'design'), an understanding of the mechanisms involved, in this case linking people and environments, is absolutely essential. There has been little, if any, research explicitly directed at identifying mechanisms. However, a first attempt to list possible mechanisms proved rather encouraging; there seem to be a limited number of them, although in time, others may be identified. Such a first list includes:

The mechanisms linking people and environments *Physiology:* adaptation, comfort with regard to temperature, humidity, light levels, glare, noise, etc.; the need for variability in temperature, humidity, etc., e.g. in air-conditioning, lighting, etc.

Anatomy: sizes and heights of elements, e.g., ergonomics and anatomical comfort; these two have implications for various handicaps and hence 'universal design.'

Perception: the sensory reception of information from the environment. This is essential; without perceiving the external (and even internal!) environment, nothing else can happen. This perception is *multi-sensory*, although designers emphasize only vision, neglecting the other sensory modalities as do 'critics.' It is also important to know how the various senses work together, and it is useful to think of perception as the integration of the various senses.

Cognition: this concerns the mental processes that intervene between perception (acquisition of information) and knowledge about the environment. There is the anthropological meaning of cognition, which concerns how the world is construed, categorized into domains and schemata, and named, i.e., how one makes sense of the world. There is also the more common psychological sense of the term, which concerns how we learn about the world, construct mental maps, orient ourselves, and navigate, i.e., how we can operate in the world.

Meaning: this is related to the anthropological aspects of cognition, includes latent aspect, and is most important (and is discussed later). It involves images, ideals, status, identity, and many other very important aspects of the environment.

Affect: the emotions, feelings, moods, etc. elicited by the environment, its sensory qualities, its meaning, etc.

Evaluation: this leads to preferences and choices based more on wants (and related to meaning and affect) than on needs. It also includes 'aesthetics,' which I identify with perceptual aspects of environmental quality (to be discussed later in Chapter 4).

Action and Behavior: the response to cognition, meaning, affect, and evaluation.

Supportiveness: this can be physiological, anatomical, psychological, social, cultural, affective, regarding choice, activity systems, behavior, and so on.

Chapter 1

Some of the components of culture: to be discussed later.

Culture and the built environment

Note that I have already had to refer to 'culture' several times. This is because culture plays an important role in all three of the basic questions. This will be discussed in more detail later in Chapter 2, Section 1. However, culture is not the *only* thing involved, which is why the relation between culture (and anthropology) and the built environment needs to be studied within the framework of EBS.

For example, as we have already seen, although Question 1 clearly includes culture, it also includes bio-social, and hence evolutionary, psychological, physiological, and other human characteristics, all of which need to be considered in relation to built environments. The number of such characteristics means that no single short book can cover even a fraction of them. This book will, therefore, consider a single, albeit broad and complex, topic: the relation between *culture* and design. This is why I changed the original suggested title of the book — *Anthropology and Architecture* — to *Culture, Architecture, and Design.*

EBS is inter-disciplinary

This change is also due to the fact that no single discipline can cover the full range of relevant human characteristics. Thus, EBS is highly interdisciplinary, i.e., many disciplines must be involved. Also, all aspects of design (including research, analysis, programming, design, and evaluation) must draw on all these disciplines. I do not question the valuable role that anthropology can and must play in the study of EBR. I personally have found some anthropological concepts and approaches useful. For example, anthropology can be linked directly to EBS through ethnographic descriptions and analyses of behavior, built environments, and material culture, their origins, uses, meanings, and so on. Through archaeology, great historical depth can be established, the temporal aspects of a large and diverse body of evidence added to the cross-cultural aspects emphasized by ethnography; ethnoarchaeology links these two domains. There can also be indirect links, with which this book is concerned — through meaning and through parts of physical anthropology to evolution and its implications for understanding humans. Many of these and other potentially valuable linkages and contributions have not yet been made or are just beginning to be made.

However, anthropology is too limited not only because of the multidisciplinary nature of EBS. Even in dealing with 'culture' (possibly the defining concept of anthropology), other disciplines need to be involved. This is because although when most people think of anthropology they think of culture, the term 'anthropology' actually means 'the study of anthropos' (humans). But anthropology cannot, and does not, study humans on its own. There are many other disciplines that do that, so that anthropology is just one among them. Without trying to be exhaustive, it is easy to list a large number of fields that study anthropos. These are, in no particular order:

- Psychology
- Sociology
- History
- Pre-History
- Human (or cultural) geography
- Human landscape and urban ecology
- Evolutionary science
- Palaeoanthropology
- Sociobiology
- Evolutionary psychology
- Brain science
- Cognitive science
- Cognitive neuroscience
- Artificial intelligence and computational approaches, generally
- Behavior genetics
- Biobehavioral sciences, psychobiology, etc.
- Economics
- Political science

Fields that study anthropos (humans)

The relevance of some of these fields only became clear recently, others are new fields, and others yet can be expected to develop.

All of these and other disciplines and their sub-fields play a role in helping to achieve an understanding of humans, including their interactions with built environments and material culture, and also of the mechanisms through which these interactions occur.

It is also the case that there are many sub-fields of anthropology, which makes it difficult to know what one means

Sub-fields of anthropology

15

when that term is used. In the U.S., the *major* divisions are physical, cultural, and linguistic anthropology and archaeology; in the U.K., the divisions are physical and social anthropology and archaeology. More concisely, the two main divisions are physical and cultural in the U.S. and physical and social in the U.K. Physical anthropology includes evolutionary anthropology and palaeoanthropology (i.e., the evolution of humans) and is increasingly more scientific using genetics (hence genetic anthropology), molecular biology, and computer methods. Cultural/social anthropology includes a large number of more specific domains. For example, in 1994 an English encyclopedia of anthropology divided the field into three major areas: humanity, culture, and social life. 'Humanity' has 11 divisions, including palaeoanthropology; linguistic anthropology; archaeology (tools and material culture); ecological anthropology (subsistence); nutrition/diet; demographics; and health. 'Culture' comprises 13 divisions dealing with symbolism (*meaning*); artifacts; technology; the built environment (which I wrote about); religion; magic and myth; ritual and performance; art; music and dance; and so on. 'Social life' (which I will later call '*social expressions of culture*') has 12 divisions, including sociality among humans and animals; rules; prohibitions and kinship; sex and gender; socialization; enculturation and the development of identity; social aspects of language use; exchange and reciprocity; politics; law; and others. Not included are applied anthropology, medical anthropology, economic anthropology, ethnoarchaeology (applying current anthropological research to archaeology), and others.

Note two things. First, there probably exist other ways of subdividing the discipline, but clearly "anthropology" includes a great variety of specific sub-fields (and new ones can, and do, develop). Second, these various, more specific sub-fields vary in how strongly and directly they relate to the built environment. How useful they are depends on the specific questions about EBR being considered.

More than one in this range of disciplines that play a role in EBS and study humans and the sub-fields of anthropology can potentially help in understanding the role of culture in EBS. Dealing with *culture* rather than anthropology, therefore, seems like a more useful approach. However, before I turn to a discussion of 'culture,' it is important to clarify the way in which I use the term 'environment' (or 'built environment') so that we are clear about how culture relates to it.

CHAPTER 2

The Nature and Types of Environments

Research, to be useful and usable, cannot remain as a series of independent empirical studies. Sometimes too many such studies may even make matters more difficult. As one example, it seems clear that the extraordinarily large research literature on housing has become counterproductive. Even researchers cannot read it all, and students and practitioners have no chance to do so. And having read all these studies, one is no further ahead — they do not 'add up,' nor can one remember them. The best way of avoiding such problems is to develop explanatory theory, which, unfortunately, EBS has not yet developed and has, in fact, neglected.

Explanatory theory

The development of explanatory theory is a lengthy process and one that cannot be accomplished by an individual; it is a communal task. One can, however, specify some of the requirements necessary before one can begin.[2] One major and essential requirement is to have some minimum amount of data. This, since its formal founding in 1969, EBS has now acquired. This is needed in order to begin to reveal patterns and regularities. It is those that one tries to explain through research and theory building; they are the start of explanatory theory.

An intermediate and early step towards theory is to begin to develop generalizations. In this, the patterns and regularities mentioned above are essential. However, for valid generalizations and in order to detect real and meaningful patterns, one needs the largest and most diverse body of evidence. This has major implications not only for how one studies environmental design (in addition to basing it on EBS research) but also for what one studies (i.e., from what environments one learns), and that has major implications for our topic of the relation between culture and the built environment.

More specifically, to enlarge and broaden the evidence used, compared with what is customary, four steps (or 'expansions') of the evidence used are needed. The first is to include the full range of types of environments — including those of prehistoric, historic, preliterate and tribal societies, vernacular and popular environments, spontaneous settlements, and so on — to add to the better known work of professionals (high-style environments). The second step involves including the full range of cultures, both present and past. The third step then involves including the full span of that past (not merely the Western tradition of the past few thousand years). This means going back to prehistory to our hominid ancestors and possibly even earlier to the evolutionary origins of both built environments and culture. The fourth step involves dealing with the whole environment, not just isolated buildings. This I will elaborate shortly.

This is clearly a very different body of evidence than is usually studied in architectural history or considered in so-called architectural 'theory.' It should be noted that the first three steps clearly involve aspects of 'culture,' whereas the fourth means that one cannot study only buildings but must include their inhabitants and their possessions and furnishings, i.e., much of *material culture*. Nor can one just study buildings in isolation but needs to consider how buildings relate as part of a system to open spaces, streets, other settings, neighborhoods, settlements, and sometimes even regions (and in all cases, their 'furnishings'). As part of that, it is also often necessary to study high-style and vernacular environments together (i.e., the relationships between them), often as they were originally. This greatly helps to understand both types of environments, and often neither can be understood in isolation.[3] It follows from the discussion immediately above that one needs clearly and explicitly to conceptualize what is meant by 'environment.'

Conceptualizing Housing

Before discussing how one might conceptualize 'environment' in general, I begin by considering a specific type of environment — housing. I will use housing as an example throughout this book, with only occasional references to other types of settings. This is, first, because all cultures and groups possess dwellings of some sort, so that one can compare them and generalize from them. Second, the dwelling is the primary setting for most people, which makes it most important. Third, it comprises the bulk of the built environment even when there are many other building types present. Fourth, it is the most typical product of vernacular design, hence, the one most influenced by culture. It also varies with culture, and the reasons for its extraordinary variability pose an important question, which leads to the role of culture, the topic of this book. This will be discussed later in Chapter 5.

I begin by pointing out that in doing any comparative research, including cross-cultural, a 'neutral' definition or conceptualization is essential. If one wants to study housing (or dwellings) cross-culturally, historically, or in other comparative ways, one cannot compare the physical artifacts encountered because they are not equivalent.

FIGURE 4.
Two different
types of houses.

BUILDING A

BUILDING B

**Comparing
systems of
settings**

The reason is that many activities that take place within the house in one case (A) may occur in a widely dispersed system of settings in the case of another house (B) (or in any other cases). The question is what activities take place where.[4] The units to be compared, therefore, are not the two houses but the systems of settings within which particular systems of activities take place (both terms will be clarified later). The same activities are selected in the cases being compared, and one identifies where they occur. Let us assume that in one case, all occur inside the house (especially during the winter in areas with severe winters); in the other case, only one might occur in the house (see Figure 5, p. 21).

After establishing the extent of the system of settings involved in case (B), the comparison is between (A) and (B) in Figure 6 on p. 21. The dwelling is then defined as a particular system of settings, and it is the dwellings that are compared.

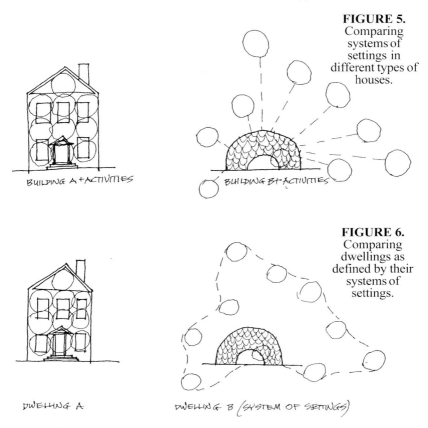

FIGURE 5. Comparing systems of settings in different types of houses.

BUILDING A + ACTIVITIES

BUILDING B + ACTIVITIES

FIGURE 6. Comparing dwellings as defined by their systems of settings.

DWELLING A

DWELLING B (SYSTEM OF SETTINGS)

This type of conceptualization makes a major difference, not only to the use of the dwelling, and thus the nature of housing, it also influences the use of streets, specialized settings, and neighborhoods. It also has implications for appraisals of density and hence crowding; this, in turn, influences the evaluation of the quality of housing with major effects on decisions about redevelopment, 'slum' clearance, etc.

For example, in the 1960s a part of Boston (The West End) was demolished and rebuilt ('redeveloped'). A major reason was that the density was deemed too high and the dwellings overcrowded. Although this was partly due to the norms and standards used (which themselves are culturally variable), the major issue was a misunderstanding of

Misunderstanding a system of settings

21

FIGURE 7.
Miscalculation of
housing density/
crowding in the
West End of
Boston, due to
ignoring the
larger system of
settings

the system of settings used by the residents. The planners' evaluations were based on dividing the area of the apartments by the number of residents in the household. However, in this particular case, many activities actually took place in a variety of other settings that were used regularly. These included stoops, streets, clubs, coffee shops, bars, and others (the whole neighborhood). When one considered people's activity systems as occurring within that larger system of settings, the dwellings were, in fact, adequate; density was not too high, and there was no overcrowding.

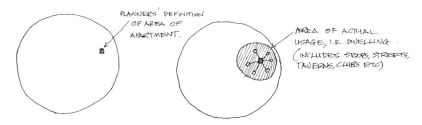

(based on verbal
description in
Hartman CW (1963)
Social values and
housing orientation.
*Journal of Social
Issues* 19(2). For
additional examples,
see Rapoport A
(1977) *Human
aspects of urban
form.* Oxford:
Pergamon, Chapter
5.).

The very different evaluation was, of course, also due to differences in the definitions by planners and users of environmental quality, privacy, desired levels of social interaction, and so on. In fact, what planners had defined as a 'slum,' the residents regarded as an area of quality and liked living there. Many *chose* to live there, and when relocated after redevelopment, they grieved for a long time. In other words, the two evaluations of the area and its environmental quality were different. This is clearly a function of the two groups, hence an aspect of culture, and will be elaborated later[5] (Chapter 5).

A system of settings is part of a larger system

Furthermore, the system of settings that is the dwelling is part of a larger system — the block or compound, neighborhood, settlement, and even larger units. These contain other settings that are important for those activity systems that are specifically or directly domestic.

Thus, once in a particular city (which is often also chosen) when people choose housing, they choose not only the house (or apartment) but also the lot or site, block, street, neighborhood, and area of the city. In fact, one typically begins with these larger-scale elements.

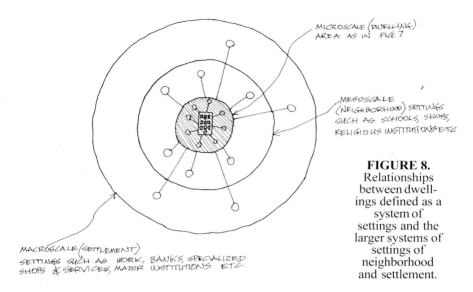

MICROSCALE (DWELLING)
AREA AS IN FIG. 7

MESOSCALE
(NEIGHBORHOOD) SETTINGS
SUCH AS SCHOOLS, SHOPS,
RELIGIOUS INSTITUTIONS ETC

MACROSCALE (SETTLEMENT)
SETTINGS SUCH AS WORK, BANKS, SPECIALIZED
SHOPS & SERVICES, MAJOR INSTITUTIONS ETC

FIGURE 8.
Relationships between dwellings defined as a system of settings and the larger systems of settings of neighborhood and settlement.

For example, a Canadian newspaper, in a special supplement for first-time house buyers, begins with the area of the city and neighborhood. Much space is devoted to many neighborhood characteristics, both positive and negative. It is pointed out that due to resource constraints, tradeoffs must typically be made between neighborhood quality and house quality. Only after this detailed discussion of location, proximity to or distance from a variety of other settings (to be defined below) and which are enumerated, characteristics of residents, noise pollution, quality of schools, real estate taxes, crime and safety, traffic, and so on are the block and the lot evaluated. Only then are the house itself and many specific, smaller-scale components of the house evaluated. Clearly it is the whole system of settings that buyers are recommended to evaluate. It is also made clear that the trade-offs, evaluations, and choices made will vary for different people (i.e., among members of different groups), which, as we will see later in Chapter 5, are themselves defined by 'culture.'

Given that systems of activities occur within such systems of settings, what does or does not happen in some settings influences what does or does not happen in others. This is closely related to *rules* about what is appropriate or inap-

Rules in systems of settings

propriate behavior in different settings (who does what, where, when, including/excluding whom, and why), and such rules are part of culture. In any case, it should be clear that not only can the two houses in Figure 4 on p. 20 not be compared but that one cannot just consider isolated, single buildings but must also consider the larger environment. The extent of that environment, defined by the extent of the relevant system of settings, needs to be discovered (not assumed): how far it extends, for whom, what specific settings are involved, the various rules operating, etc. This applies not only to house choice but to any specific activity. As one example, in a case where a children's playground in a housing project was not being used, the researchers began with the activity — play — and traced the system of settings where children actually played; it was quite extensive.

Four conceptualizations of environment

This conceptualization of the environment as a system of settings is just one of four conceptualizations that I find most useful; undoubtedly others could be developed. They are listed starting with the most abstract, and hence most complex, to the most concrete and therefore simplest; all are influenced by 'culture.' They are also complementary, not conflicting or contradictory; which is most 'useful' depends on whether one is doing research or designing, the question being considered, etc. The environment can be understood as:

(a) The organization of space, time, meaning, and communication
(b) A system of settings (already briefly discussed)
(c) The cultural landscape
(d) Consisting of fixed, semi-fixed, and non-fixed elements.

Despite the different levels of abstraction and complexity of these formulations, they can be unified. The most fundamental and abstract formulation (the environment as the organization of space, time, meaning, and communication) is expressed physically as cultural landscapes at various scales, from the region, through townscape to the housescape. Cultural landscapes consist of systems of settings, within which systems of activities take place. The cultural landscape, the elements comprising settings and their cues, and the activity systems are made up of fixed and semi-fixed elements, and both are created and occupied by non-fixed elements (mainly people). Thus, the four formulations are not only complementary, but closely linked. However, each of the formulations (or conceptualizations) needs to be discussed briefly.

(a) The importance of this formulation is that it goes beyond merely 'space,' which designers tend to emphasize to the exclusion of other aspects.[6] It introduces *time*, which is most important because people live in time as much as in space. Human activities are organized in time — day/night, weekday/weekend, workday/rest-day, mundane/sacred, etc. — and many consequences follow: images of the same city differ at different times; privacy can be achieved by organizing activities in time, as well as through spatial separation, physical devices, and other (culturally specific) mechanisms. Cultural differences in the organization of time may lead to more conflicts or difficulties than space organization (late dinner, and hence late noise, among early-to-bed people; the effect of siesta on the closure of shops or banks at other people's working time, etc.).

The organization of space, time, meaning, and communication

Also introduced is *meaning,* normally neglected or seen as something added to "function" rather than as a (the?) most important aspect of function and a critical element in wants, evaluation, and preference of environments and many of its characteristics — ambience, color, materials, styles, and so on. Human activities and interaction (i.e., communication) also follow naturally, and hence boundaries, cues, transitions, rule systems, inclusion/exclusion of certain people, etc. These are part of, but separable from, space organization. Also included is the specific nature of the rules (based on ideals, norms, etc.) used in organizing communication; these vary, particularly with culture. In fact, rules partly help to define groups (people who share rules) that, as we will see later, are an important aspect of culture. Rules also guide behavior and play a central role in lifestyles and activity systems. They are reflected in the choices made in the design process ('the choice model of design' discussed later in Chapter 4). How settings work is also determined by the relevant rules and communicated by cues. Rules also explain how cultural landscapes come to be, as I will discuss below. Note also that conceptualizing the environment in this way cuts across scales, from regions to the furnishing of interiors.

Chapter 2

A system of settings

FIGURE 9.
Navajo hogan showing known (and, at best, subtly marked) named settings, which have symbolic and ritual significance. The whole hogan is sacred and structured through sacred directions, movement, etc., i.e., sacred meanings (see Rapoport A (1969) The pueblo and the hogan. In P Oliver (Ed.), *Shelter and society*. London: Barrie and Rockliff, pp. 66-79, esp. p. 75.).

(b) An example of the conceptualization of the environment as a system of settings has already been introduced in the discussion about the nature of 'dwellings.' It now needs to be generalized and developed, beginning with the concept of "setting."

A setting comprises a milieu, which defines a situation within which ongoing (i.e., regular) and predictable behavior occurs. The boundaries of that milieu, how they are marked, by whom they are penetrated, and so on, vary with culture. Settings are thus culturally variable. By using what is called the 'dramaturgical analogy,' one can also think of a setting as a stage on which people act and play various roles. The milieu and the behavior in it are linked by rules as to what is appropriate and expected in the setting. These rules are specific to the setting and the situation that it defines; appropriate behavior is defined by the situation. All of these phenomena are culturally extremely variable. Thus, activities which occur in settings that are clearly separated in, say, the United States, may all occur in a single setting in many traditional cultures. These 'work' because of clear, consistent, and strong rules about location and seating patterns for various people; cues can be very subtle or knowledge alone may be sufficient.

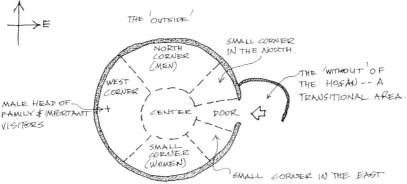

As rules change, so do settings

The link between rules, behavior, and culture means that as cultural rules change, so do the activities appropriate to various settings and also the cues. This is important both for understanding cultural differences and for situations of culture change (especially rapid culture change) common today and, therefore, for design — for example, in housing. Changes in rules may be temporary, as when a street changes from a setting for traffic into one for a street (or, as it is called in the U.S., block) party, a setting for play, games, social interaction, cooking, eating and drinking, and so on. Similarly, an open space can be an outdoor market, a soccer field, a playground, or a venue for a political rally; only the rules change. Many permanent differences in rules account for the major contrasts among street activities, for example, between say the United States (especially in suburbs) as compared to Spain and, even more, India.

For example, in many areas of the United States (especially residential areas where other uses are excluded) empty quiet streets are the ideal and the norm. Very few, if any, activities, except children playing or jogging and walking, are appropriate and, in some areas, even the latter two are frowned upon. In India there is a dense, bewildering mix of activities at a very fine grain and correspondingly diverse sounds, smells, and sights. There is a mixture of animals, people, bicycles, rickshaws, cars, trucks, and buses. The streets are full of a great variety of people in all sorts of costumes not only walking or riding but also standing, sitting, squatting, lying down, sleeping, cooking, eating, getting their hair cut or being shaved, doing laundry, fixing bicycles or tires, manufacturing things, sewing, playing, chanting, arguing, begging, performing, bargaining, and even praying.

It is important to emphasize that settings are not the same as spaces. One space may contain many settings, i.e., a space may contain different settings at one time.

FIGURE 10A.
Different settings
in space.

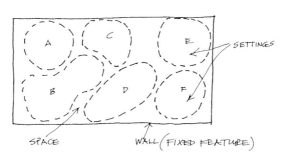

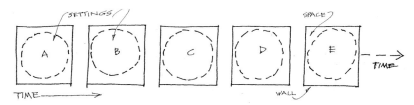

FIGURE 10B.
Different settings
in time.

The same space can also become different settings at different times, as with the temporary changes in rules already discussed: timetables and scheduling of rooms, for example, as at a university. Settings are also not the same as neighborhoods, streets, buildings, or even rooms. Any one of these may contain a number of settings, at larger scales many hundreds. For example, a city block in the U.S. had over 1000; 3 blocks of a street in Taipei, Taiwan (excluding settings in adjoining buildings) had almost 400, mainly vendors.

Settings and their rules are usually communicated by cues, which are the physical elements of the setting and its 'furnishings' (see (d) below). These act as mnemonics, reminding people about the situation and hence about appropriate behavior, making effective co-action among occupants possible. One can think of the cues as denoting a 'frame,' which in turn elicits a 'script' — a repertoire of appropriate actions and behaviors. This is a process whereby people constantly change their behavior as they move among settings — dwelling, restaurant, library, concert, etc. — and as their roles change — host or guest in a house, diner or waiter in a restaurant. In order to be effective (i.e., to 'work'), cues need first to be noticed; they cannot be too subtle, a frequent failing in design, so that perception, redundancy, etc. need to be considered. In traditional societies, because the rules are so clear, very subtle cues, or even just knowledge, is enough. Today, however, very clear and strong cues are necessary in order to work. Second, cues then need to be understood. This is an aspect of culture. Cues that do not match cultural schemata and draw on tacit cultural knowledge are meaningless and do not work. Of course, those involved must also be prepared to 'obey,' i.e., to follow the expected and appropriate behavior. Although this is not as 'automatic' as in traditional societies, it is still surprisingly common, as is shown by cultural differences and changed behavior by individuals as they

change settings. In any case, unlike noticing and understanding, which designers can ensure using knowledge from
EBS, whether people obey cues is outside designers' control.

As we have already seen in the case of dwellings, settings
cannot be considered singly but are organized into systems, within which systems of activities take place. The
organization of both is culturally variable. Thus, settings
are connected in varying complex ways not only in space,
in terms of their proximities, linkages and separations,
boundaries, etc., but also in time, in terms of their sequen-
tial ordering (see Figure 11, p. 30).

Also variable is their centrality, the rules that apply, who
is included or excluded, how deeply one penetrates, etc.
These are, once again, culturally variable. It follows that
the extent of the system, the settings of which it is composed, and its organization cannot be assumed but need to
be discovered. It also follows (as we have seen in the discussion of housing) that what happens or does not happen
in some settings greatly influences what happens or does
not happen in others.

It is also important to note that the complexity of systems
of settings evolves. This happens with so-called 'modernization' of developing countries and, more generally, as
societies become larger and more complex and the number of distinct, separated, specialized settings goes up. In a
tribal society, a single house space may be many settings
and, in addition to houses, there may be very few other
settings. In modern cities, as we have already seen, there
are large numbers of very specialized settings — many
kinds of buildings, dining places, shops, offices, classrooms, and so on. Even in houses (let alone dwellings)
there are many distinct settings — porch, entry, corridor,
living room, dining room, master bedroom, bedroom, study,
family room, kitchen, bathroom, laundry, toilet, pantry,
closets and other storage, basement (itself subdivided),
attic, and so on (note that the presence of such settings
and their names are culture-specific). How settings are related in space and time also becomes more complex.

(c) The concept 'cultural landscape' comes from cultural geography. It refers to the results of the interaction
between human actions and the 'primeval' landscape over

**The 'cultural
landscape'**

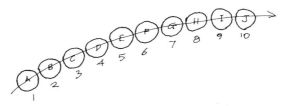

USA: SEQUENCE OF SETTINGS BASED ON PROXIMITY/EFFICIENCY. STRONG INSTRUMENTAL EMPHASIS; LOW LEVEL MEANINGS PREDOMINATE.

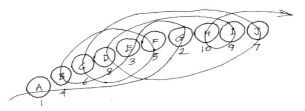

INDONESIA: (EG RAMADAN FAMILY VISITS). SEQUENCE OF SETTINGS BASED ON SOCIAL & STATUS RELATIONSHIPS; MIDDLE LEVEL MEANINGS PREDOMINATE.

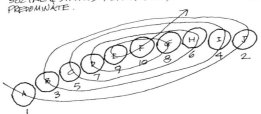

AUSTRALIAN ABORIGINES: (EG RETRACING 'DREAMTIME' TREKS). SEQUENCE OF SETTINGS IS BASED ON RITUAL MOVEMENTS & SACRED RELATIONSHIPS; LATENT/HIGH LEVEL MEANINGS PREDOMINATE.

FIGURE 11. Hypothetical sequences of visits to a series of settings in different cultures (from Rapoport A (1990) Systems of settings and systems of activities. In S Kent (Ed.), *Domestic architecture and the use of space*. Cambridge: Cambridge University Press, pp. 9-20; Fig. 2.4, p. 14.).

time. One can ask at what point 'primeval' becomes 'cultural,' i.e., how much human impact is necessary before some threshold or transition is reached. Clearly the more modified by humans, the more 'cultural' does a landscape become. Those most modified — settlements — are cultural landscapes *par excellence*. Yet even hunters and gatherers modify the landscape considerably through hunting, gathering, fire, etc. Thus, Australia (before contact) and the Amazon jungle represent cultural landscapes. Similarly, pastoralists have shaped landscape, for example, through the impact of goats in the Mediterranean region or of cows on high Alpine meadows in Switzerland.

Human modification of the landscape, however, became much clearer after the advent of agriculture. The gardens of the New Guinea highlands, the rice terraces of Asia, the olive tree terraces of parts of the Mediterranean region, the date tree oases of North Africa and the Middle East are as much cultural landscapes as the dwellings and settlements in their midst; moreover, they form a single system. This emphasizes the importance of relationships in the environment at various scales: 'natural' landscape, settlement areas, neighborhoods, buildings, open spaces, etc. In places like New Zealand (and parts of Australia), the whole landscape was transformed through the introduction not only of buildings and settlements but also exotic plants, transforming the country. This was reinforced by many introduced names referring to Europe. Thus, what we typically call 'natural' landscapes are really cultural but are composed of 'natural' materials — plants, soil, rocks, water, etc. — whereas settlements consist mainly of man-made materials or elements, and even vegetation and water often appear to be more 'cultural.' The difference is the *degree* of modification, but they are all cultural landscapes. This also emphasizes the unity of design; landscape architecture, urban design, architecture, and interior design merely deal with different parts of a single system. An important aspect of cultural landscapes is that they are not 'designed' in the traditional sense of the term, or only small parts of them are. They are the result of innumerable independent decisions by many people over long periods of time. Yet they have distinct character and, if one knows the cues, a single image may be enough to identify them. A most important question is how these apparently independent decisions can form such clearly recognizable wholes. The most likely answer is that people make their choices, i.e., modify the landscape, following shared schemata, notions of ideal people leading ideal lives in ideal environments. These schemata are cultural.

Fixed, semi-fixed, and non-fixed elements

(d) The most concrete, and hence simplest, conceptualization of 'environment' is that it is composed of fixed, semi-fixed, and non-fixed elements. Fixed elements are infrastructure, buildings, walls, floors, ceilings, columns, etc.; although they do change, they do so relatively infrequently, and hence slowly. Semi-fixed elements are the 'furnishings' of the environment, interior or exterior. At the urban scale they are trees and gardens, fences, signs, billboards, lights, benches, kiosks, etc.; in buildings they are furniture, decorations and ornaments, plants, curtains or blinds, etc. Non-fixed elements are typically people and their activities, behaviors, clothing and hairstyles, and also vehicles and animals. This again immediately includes behavior, social interaction and communication, activity systems, rule systems, etc. as part of the environment, and indirectly relates environments to values, ideals, tastes, wants, etc. It also links settlements and buildings to all landscapes and to all kinds of outdoor and indoor furnishings at all scales.

Note that settings guide behavior (i.e., the non-fixed elements (us!)) not only, or even principally, through the fixed-feature elements of architecture but through semi-fixed elements that provide essential (and increasingly important) cues. Other people present, and their activities and behaviors, are also very important cues, often used when the fixed and semi-fixed elements are not noticed (too subtle, not redundant enough) or not understood (culturally inappropriate). The importance of semi-fixed elements has important design implication: built environments (whether at the urban or building scale) will always contain many semi-fixed elements, and these need to be allowed for (see the discussion of open-endedness later in the postscript). Also, since few people create their own environments now, or have them created, they possess, define, and modify settings through manipulating semi-fixed elements. This process is often called 'personalization;' the culture-(group-) specific nature of such elements often gives places their ambience (if the people are homogeneous in their values, tastes, etc., i.e., in their culture). Also, the elements used and their organization are often at odds with designers' tastes or values, leading to conflicts. This can be at small scales, such as interior decorations, garden ornaments (gnomes, pink flamingos), or at large scales — as signs and billboards.

Note that in my earlier example of an open space becoming an outdoor market, minimally, there is knowledge related to temporal organization: At a given time, people congregate to play their appropriate roles in the situation 'market.' However, the very presence of displays of goods for sale — semi-fixed elements — inevitably provides cues. Even more frequently, however, other semi-fixed elements play an important role as cues: awnings, umbrellas, stands, carts, etc. When these (and the people) disappear, the space is ready to become another setting with different rules — playground, soccer game, performance, etc. — often again marked by semi-fixed elements.

The importance of semi-fixed elements in defining settings, and thus guiding behavior, can be shown through examples. I will give two.

(1) Consider a classroom. First, note that one needs cultural knowledge even to know the concept of 'classroom' and its uses and, thus, how to behave. By rearranging the furniture and adding other cues, the same room (fixed feature) can become different settings, including ones not commonly identified with classrooms; behaviors will change accordingly. This is a kind of 'mental experiment.'

FIGURE 12. Different settings in a 'classroom.'

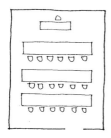

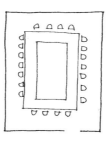

CLASSROOM-LECTURE   CLASSROOM-SEMINAR   CLASSROOM - END OF TERM PARTY

33

(2) Consider a house and the many specialized settings already described. Some are identified by location; in a given culture there is a consistent arrangement and ordering of such settings. But, importantly, it is semi-fixed elements that provide the cues that identify the various settings and communicate (highly culture-specific) rules about appropriate behavior. In another 'mental experiment,' take a room and change its furnishings; it is those that clearly identify the various settings.

FIGURE 13. Note that the settings themselves are culture-specific. In addition, the organization of the semi-fixed elements and their nature, defining any given setting, also vary cross-culturally.

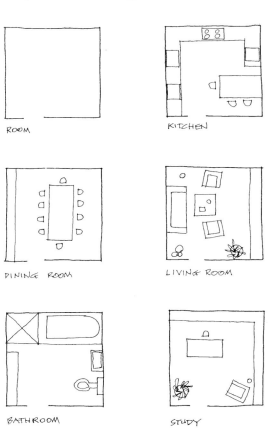

ROOM

KITCHEN

DINING ROOM

LIVING ROOM

BATHROOM

STUDY

In all these cases, one needs to have the schema for 'living room,' 'dining room,' etc. (as for 'classroom'), and these schemata vary cross-culturally, as do the nature and arrangement of the semi-fixed elements. Also, in my discussion so far, I have mentioned cultural variability in connection with many aspects of the environment. Thus, the time has come to begin discussing culture and its importance, role, etc., how one might define or conceptualize 'culture,' and how one can use the concept. I begin with the importance of culture.

CHAPTER 3

The Importance of Culture

The major premise of this book is that within an EBS context, a consideration and an understanding of culture are extremely important in many domains, including environmental design. It should be emphasized that this is an *hypothesis*. In reality, the importance of culture cannot be assumed or asserted but needs to be tested empirically. Moreover, it also needs to be established how important culture is in various domains, how important relative to other considerations in environmental design, for whom, under what circumstances, for which environments, and so on. These are all empirical questions, but I will provisionally accept this hypothesis because it seems to be well supported by the available evidence.

The General Importance of Culture

In connection with EBS, culture is important in two ways: first, in identifying the role of culture in various explanations, models, and eventually theories of EBR, i.e., its role in the discipline as a whole; and second, more closely related to environmental design, how important culture is in understanding particular specific user groups, situations, and environments. Regarding the first, I have already suggested that culture clearly seems to play a role in all three of the basic questions of EBS and is, therefore, inescapable, a point I will elaborate shortly. As a result, and in response to the role in specific issues of design, there has been, and continues to be, major growth in the interest in culture and a growing awareness of its importance, or at least of investigating it, e.g., since *House Form and Culture* in 1969. Similarly, a concern with culture has become ever more important in many other fields:

Fields in which culture has become important
- Developmental psychology
- Adolescence
- Developmental disorders
- Language development
- Counseling

36

- Education (learning and teaching)
- Psychology
- Sports
- Economics
- Business
- Organizational behavior
- Work/employment
- Marketing and advertising
- Product development and packaging
- Law
- Politics
- Strategy, and military and security studies
- Third world development (economic, social, physical)
- Psychiatry
- Substance abuse
- Medicine and health, generally
- Human ecology, use of resources and sustainability
- Aging, etc.

A number of these have potential links to environmental design. For example, once health and medicine are studied in different groups (and, as we shall see, groups are a key aspect of culture), this leads to a concern with ideals, values, lifestyle, religion, sex and other roles, etc. We will see that these are closely related to what we call 'culture.' They also suggest the need to design specific health delivery systems, sometimes considering the potential role of traditional medicine and healers, and possibly the need to design health facilities (clinics, hospitals, etc.) differently for different groups.

Returning to the *general* importance of culture in EBS, I will elaborate the role that culture plays in the three basic questions. It is that role which made me suggest earlier that a consideration of culture is inescapable in EBS and environmental design. First of all, the possession of culture is what is generally taken to define humans; since EBS involves humans, one must consider culture. At the same time, the specifics of culture lead to major differences among various groups. This results in a paradox: the possession of culture makes us all human and defines our species, yet it also divides us by language, religion, food habits, rules, and many other specific aspects of culture to the extent that one can speak of 'pseudo-species.'

Characteristics of people are related to culture

It follows that many important characteristics of people (Question 1) are related to culture.

Effects of environment on people

Similar environments can have very different effects on people (Question 2), depending on their specific characteristics, many of which, as we have just seen, are cultural or influenced by culture. For example, for sedentary groups, being displaced presents severe problems; for nomads, it is being settled. High-rise apartments have a very negative effect on members of some groups but work well for others. Density and crowding mean very different things to members of different groups so that the same standards cannot be used, and similar numbers of dwellings per unit area, or people per dwelling will be evaluated very differently and, therefore, have different consequences. The contexts or circumstances also play an important role in the effects environments have on people, and many of these are related to culture. For example, rates of cultural change are important, with rapid change often presenting problems. Another factor is the 'cognitive distance' among groups, so that urbanization is easier for settled people than nomads, and migration easier when cultures are more similar. Another important contextual variable related to the two just mentioned is what is called 'reduced competence' and hence higher criticality.

'Reduced competence' (a technical term) refers to the notion that people, due to age, illness, extremely rapid, and hence disruptive, rates of cultural and social change with the consequent need to acculturate to very different lifestyles, work, time, organization, etc., have fewer resources available to them than others. This reduces their ability to cope with the additional demands imposed by unsuitable, unsupportive environments. Such demands, with which fully competent people can deal easily, may become destructive for more vulnerable people who have already reached (or even exceeded) the limit of their ability to cope. It follows that environments have much larger effects on people like these. This may be because they cannot leave unsuitable environments and seek out others (blocked habitat selection). It may also be because they cannot rely on various customary social and cultural mechanisms. In either case, the criticality of environments is increased and highly supportive (possibly even 'prosthetic') environments are needed. Note that such supportiveness is often indirect (as discussed in Chapter 1 regarding basic question 2) and often through various social and other expressions or components of culture, to be discussed later in Chapter 5.

Note also that many of the mechanisms linking people and environments (Question 3) are cultural, are related to culture, or vary with culture. This variability differs for different mechanisms. I have already suggested that there seems to be a limited number of such mechanisms. A first attempt to list possible mechanisms, knowledge of which is essential for explanation of EBR (and hence explanatory theory), has already been given in Chapter 1.

Cultural mechanisms linking people and environment

Two things need to be noted. First, some of these mechanisms vary much more with culture than others. For example, whereas perception is largely unaffected by culture, cognition varies significantly with culture, and meaning and evaluation are culturally extremely variable. Second, some of these mechanisms interact and work together, for example, affect, meaning, and evaluation. Also, this list is a first effort and can be expanded (or modified) if necessary, i.e., as and if new mechanisms are discovered and new knowledge obtained. Also, the mechanisms listed can be further subdivided, for example, meaning into different levels and types, the ideal images involved, etc., or by listing the specifics of cultural aspects of supportiveness. This implies that even more specific and concrete mechanisms can be introduced, often on the basis of new findings. One example is specific brain mechanisms for various cognitive tasks, such as way-finding, orientation, memory, learning, affect, etc., discovered by cognitive neuroscience, which is developing extremely fast. Another example is that new theoretical developments can also make mechanisms more specific. Thus, my interpretation of one behavioral mechanism, how settings communicate expected behaviors via cues, is clarified by frame/script theory from computation science, which shows how this process actually works.[7]

There is another formulation of the domain of EBS.[8] This suggests that EBS is concerned with settings and places, user groups, and socio-behavioral phenomena. This formulation can be derived from that based on the three basic questions, which therefore I see as more basic and fundamental. More important for the present topic is the fact that all three are, once again, related to culture. Different

User groups

groups subdivide the world into different domains and settings and use them differently (this also applies to 'places,' but that is a term which I believe has many problems and which I will, therefore, not use). User groups are generally, and most usefully, defined through 'culture' (as we will see later), and many socio-behavioral phenomena are related to, influenced by, or defined by 'culture.'

The discussion thus far suggests, as already pointed out, that groups seem to be the key. For example, users as a whole are very different indeed from designers, and this difference between these two groups, which, in effect, are different (sub)cultures, creates many of the problems EBS is meant to alleviate, which are discussed below. Also, users are *not* one group; there are many user groups, defined by various specific characteristics important for culture-specific environmental design; this bears on the *specific* importance of culture in EBS, as opposed to its general importance, which I have been discussing. The nature of relevant groups is an under-researched topic, but those often used in design and even in EBS (e.g., the elderly, children, patients, the urban poor of the Third World, etc.) are *not* useful because they are much too broad. This topic will be discussed in detail later in Chapter 6 and is an important aspect of this book.

The Variability of Environments

There is a very important question: Why should there be such an extraordinary variety of built environments, especially houses and dwellings, and also settlement forms? This variety has previously not been explicitly noted nor emphasized. The recent publication of the *Encyclopedia of Vernacular Architecture of the World* suggests the possibility of an estimate. In it, I counted 1,278 areas/groups, each with its own distinct environment. Others exist, because the coverage, although extraordinary, is not complete. Also, the coverage is by groups and areas, some of which comprise more than one type (and form) of environment. Other classifications are also possible, which might further increase the number of house types, settlement forms, non-domestic buildings, significant outdoor settings, etc. Moreover, any one of the entries in the encyclopedia could be studied at a finer grain or scale, leading to more types.

This extraordinary variety is puzzling because, after all, people do a much more limited set of things in such environments, and the number of climatic zones, materials, and techniques is also smaller. The reference above to 'doing things' in environments and the definition of housing in Chapter 1 suggest that it is something about *activities* that results in this variety. The answer follows from the fact that activities can and need to be dismantled. In fact, activities (and this also applies to 'function') can be dismantled into four components:

- The activity itself
- How it is carried out
- How it is associated with other activities to form systems of activities
- The meaning of the activity

Four components of activities

The first is the instrumental, or manifest (i.e., obvious or self-evident), aspect of the activity; the last is its latent aspects. The important thing to note is that variability goes up as one moves from the instrumental/manifest to the latent aspects of an activity (or function).

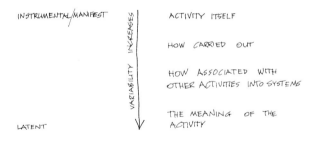

FIGURE 14. Dismantling activities.

Several examples of such an analysis of activities may help to clarify this point. Consider cooking. At its simplest, most instrumental level, cooking is the transformation of raw food into cooked food (as the title of Lévi-Strauss's well-known book suggests). It is a particularly useful activity to consider for several reasons. First, because it is a human universal and hence useful for cross-cultural comparison. This universality is why Lévi-Strauss used cooking as a major discriminant between 'culture' and 'nature,' between human and non-human. This is an apparently simple activity, but because activities are an expression of lifestyle

Examples of variability in activities — cooking

(and, ultimately, of culture) and because they vary as one moves from their instrumental/manifest to their latent aspects, even this apparently simple activity is highly variable and, therefore, leads to highly variable design requirements. How food is transformed already varies a great deal: roasting, boiling, frying, baking, and other ways of applying heat (burying with rocks, throwing on the fire, a great variety of oven types even in one country, e.g., Egypt). There are also other ways of transforming food: fermenting, pickling (e.g., Kimchi in Korea), marinating, etc. Cooking containers and appliances vary a great deal, so does their location, and hence ergonomics and body positions (e.g., squatting).

Associated activities vary even more. Cooking can be a solitary activity, carried out by servants, a communal activity, a social activity, or a teaching activity for offspring. It may be accompanied by radio, music, TV, or socializing. It may be highly private, done out of sight (as in the kitchens described as "hidden rooms" in Kenya), or central in the dwelling as a place for social interaction, hospitality and entertaining, eating, and other activities. They then need to be large, as in the 'family room' in U.S. dwellings. It can also be a principal locale for most activities, including children's homework, as among the English working class. It takes on added importance when cooking becomes a hobby (gourmet cooking), a way of establishing identity, or even a status symbol.

Consider the latter in somewhat more detail. One study of Puerto Rican immigrants in New York did a redesign of tenement apartments based on architectural criteria. Since the apartments were small, efficiency kitchens were used. The activities involved were then analyzed. In this particular case, kitchens needed to be large because a specific way of cooking in front of female guests establishes female status hierarchies. In effect, cooking becomes a *performance* and effort is emphasized. Also, large groups are entertained. The large kitchen size is also made necessary by the presence of many appliances, which also help establish status. The initial design of an efficiency kitchen was totally inappropriate and an expression of Anglo-American culture where food magically appears without apparent effort.[9]

Cooking may also be linked to specific rituals (as among the Apache) or religion more generally, for example,

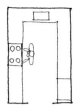

EFFICIENCY
KITCHEN

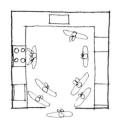

KITCHEN NEEDED

FIGURE 15.
Culturally appropriate kitchen for Puerto-Ricans in New York (based on verbal description in Zeisel J (1973) Symbolic meaning of space and the physical dimension of social relations. In J Walton and DE Carns (Eds.), *Cities in change — Studies on the urban condition.* Boston: Allyn and Bacon, pp. 252-263.).

through purity laws in India and Indians elsewhere (e.g., Singapore), which influence the relation of the kitchen to other spaces. Other examples include Orthodox Judaism where, because of requirements for separating meat and milk, kitchens need two sets of everything; polygamous Mormons require multiple kitchens, one for each wife, as do many traditional African polygamous groups.

As we have already seen, all these variations are directly related to and influence the settings involved. These can be part of a single multi-setting space (also used for many other activities, either simultaneously or organized in time), they can be a separate structure, or they can be part of the dwelling in the winter and separated in the summer, as in North Africa and the Middle East. They can be outdoors or they can be demarcated within the dwelling by walls as a 'kitchen,' itself a culture-specific concept. This latter is an example of the point already made that, in general, the number of specialized settings increases as societies become more complex. The size, nature, and organization of kitchens clearly varies depending on the more latent aspects of cooking, i.e., specific ways of cooking, associated activities, and the meaning of cooking.

One could elaborate the analysis of this single activity further and give many examples. The point is, however, that lifestyle and the latent aspects of activities (both a function of culture) can easily be linked to the built environment and design. It follows that as meanings and lifestyles change, and even as new appliances appear, kitchens change. Thus, it was recently pointed out that in South Korea, due to changes in lifestyle, kitchens needed to change in major ways. The main point is that lifestyle and

43

the latent aspects of apparently simple activities clarify reasons for the organization of built environments and are easily linked to design. This applies to all activities, no matter how apparently simple.

Variability of eating

Eating, another universal, is also highly variable in terms of foods acceptable and used (usually only a portion of those available). In fact, the choices made are often used to establish cultural, religious, ideological, and other forms of group identity. The order in which dishes are eaten also has latent meaning so that the anthropologist Mary Douglas was able to speak of "deciphering a meal." Eating can be done by individuals at odd times, by various individuals in sequence, or can become a social, family, or even ritual occasion. Who eats with whom, where, when, including/excluding whom varies with culture and plays an important role in the enculturation (socialization) of children, i.e., the transmission of culture (as does the organization and use of dwellings and other settings). It also greatly influences the design of dwellings. Thus, in Kenya and other parts of Africa, eating is also a "hidden" activity, whereas among the Apache, for example, not only does the kitchen need to be large (in one case 22 x 15 feet, i.e., ~7 x 5 meters) (as in the case of Puerto Ricans), since cooking involves a number of women, but also the living/dining room (and the distinction or separation is undesirable). The anthropologist George Esber points out that in the Apache case, three variables are involved: the extent of conversation, social distance, and the presence or absence of food. He describes complex and, for Anglo-Americans, unusual patterns that require very different organizations and allocations of space based on the behavior in settings involved. Communal meals are very important culturally and socially. Arriving guests sit on the periphery of the room at large personal distances and remain largely silent observing each other. Small rooms interfere with this pattern, making normal, i.e., expected, social interaction impossible. As a sign of welcome, women begin to prepare food. When the food is served, people gather at the table and conversation begins. (See Figure 16, p. 45.)

Similarly, living rooms — their size, significance, and formality — vary depending on latent aspects of activities. In some cases, the living room has been described as a "sacred space" and plans in which entry is directly into the living room are unsuitable; the living room needs to be

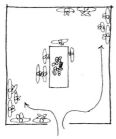

TIME 1   TIME 2   TIME 3

distant from entry. In the Danish outdoor museum of vernacular architecture, there is a very small sea-captain's cottage, half of which is a formal living room used rarely. Currently, as house sizes in the U.S. are going up (while family size goes down), living rooms tend to disappear or become mere vestiges. The way living rooms are furnished may become symbols of identity, as in what has been described (by Jopling) as a culture-specific 'aesthetic complex' among Puerto Rican immigrants in Boston.

FIGURE 16. Culture-specific use of kitchen among Apache (based on verbal description in Esber GS (1972) Indian housing for Indians. *The Kiva* Spring:141-147.).

Variability of buying and selling

Consider another activity, buying and selling, including shopping. At its most instrumental, it involves exchanging goods for other goods, in our case (and often elsewhere) through some medium of exchange (money). It can be carried out by mobile vendors, in outdoor markets, bazaars, or shops. Bargaining may be central or not acceptable. Buying and selling may be associated with important social interactions, as in specialized shops for various immigrant groups, which become central social settings in the system. They may also play a critical (latent) role of information exchange. Thus, in a case in Mexico that I have described elsewhere, periodic (e.g., weekly) outdoor markets involving mobile vendors were replaced by shops and supermarkets by planners. For often illiterate residents, the vendors acted as major sources of information and maintained communication among family members and friends; as a result, they could not be dispensed with. A combination of such markets and shops/supermarkets (to foster competition) proved to be the best solution.

Shopping may be combined with entertainment, e.g., story and fortune tellers, musicians, snake charmers, jugglers, etc., as in outdoor markets in India or the Jemaa el Fna Square in Marrakesh, Morocco. It may be an unimportant activity (servants doing it) or a very important activity in terms of status, or in itself a form of entertainment ('going shopping') and combined with lunch, afternoon tea, and the like. Shopping may be done by women, or not allowed to women and instead done by men (as in certain Islamic countries).

The settings are equally variable and, again, increase in number and specialization with increasing social complexity. There may only be periodic outdoor markets, or shops of many kinds: groceries, butchers, hardware stores, supermarkets, department stores, discount stores, boutiques, and so on. They may be organized in bazaars along streets or as shopping centers. These latter then often take on latent functions — places to 'hang out' by teenagers, to exercise (e.g., walking) by elderly, or to eat. They have been described as "new downtowns."

In this last example, I have moved from the single dwelling to other settings in the system. The shop can be a social center, as in the *bodegas* in Hispanic immigrant areas in the U.S. The pub (U.K.) or tavern (U.S.) become central settings in working class men's housing systems, in effect their 'living room.' Similar is the centrality of small wine-drinking settings in Austrian villages, tea rooms in Korea, and coffee shops in many locales. All of these become essential parts of the housing (and other) systems and play 'unexpected' roles, and 'unexpected' activities take place in them.

Discovering latent aspects of activities and settings

It follows that in all cases, the settings involved, and the activities in them, need to be *discovered*, especially since they are frequently counter-intuitive. Frequently, settings for socialization may not be those designed. Thus, in housing for the elderly, clotheslines or mail boxes may play that role. In student housing, laundry rooms and mail boxes are used, not lounges; to sit in a lounge is to admit that one lacks social links. Similarly, instead of singles bars and the like, laundromats are often used to meet members of the opposite sex, with frequent small loads maximizing opportunities. For other lifestyle groups, bookshops, galleries, and museums play similar roles; their latent aspects become important. The main purpose of gardening in front of a house may be to meet and interact with people without seeming to need it (as Gehl found in Melbourne, Australia). In all these cases, the latent aspects of activities, which are most influenced by 'culture,' greatly influence the use of settings, their location, relationships among them, and the extent of the system. This type of analysis helps answer the important question: Who does what, where, when, why, and including/excluding whom?

Consider two particularly counter-intuitive examples in somewhat more detail. In Hungarian villages, it was found (by Fel and Hofer) that important male gatherings, at which most important decisions were made, took place in the *stables* of various important men. The social system of the village was crucially linked with the presence and location of these stables, and they were used in systematic sequence. Without knowing that, the system of settings could not be understood, and it is highly unlikely that *a priori* this critical role of stables would be considered. In Nantucket (U.S.), the *garbage dump* served as the main social center of the community, as was discovered when the dump was closed.

Finally, consider an activity (play) to emphasize the importance not only of latent functions and their settings but also of identifying the extent of the system. Both examples to be discussed begin with the observation that the settings designed for play are not being used. In one example, in an Italian-American neighborhood, basketball courts were not being used. Teenage boys played basketball near shops. The reason was that prowess in basketball was important in impressing teenage girls. These, in turn, were expected by their mothers to mind babies, and they did so while socializing outside shops. Basketball thus had the latent function of male status, courtship, etc., and its location depended on the location of a particular female-activity subsystem. In the second case in a housing project, playgrounds were not being used. To analyze the situation, the activity system — children's play — was studied in terms of where it occurred. It was found that children used a wide variety of settings — streets, ditches, empty lots, wooded areas, creeks, and parking lots. The activity could only be understood by discovering the extent of the system of settings in which the system of activities (play) took place.

The extent of such systems varies with 'culture.' For example, in some situations men and women have systems of very different extent, in others there may be no difference. Typically, the systems of girls are smaller than those

The extent of systems of settings

of boys. There are age differences, the extent of systems reaching a peak at certain ages and being smaller at earlier and later ages. The nature of the environment plays a role; currently, the extent of children's play in neighborhoods in large cities is smaller than in the past because of traffic and safety concerns. Generally, such systems of settings tend to be larger in small towns. Occupation, income, education, lifestyle, and the like influence the extent of systems of settings. In some cases (e.g., in the U.S.), higher income groups use more extensive systems, in others (e.g., some developing countries), it is low-income people who do so.

'Meaning' is the most latent aspect of activity

To summarize, it is the great variability of latent aspects of activities that leads to the variety of settings for these activities and of systems of settings for systems of activities. This in turn leads to the variability of environments, such as dwelling types. In responding to the latent aspects of activity systems, they are also responding to those most closely linked to and most affected by 'culture.' Since meaning is the most latent aspect of any activity, this means that meaning is not something added to 'function' but that meaning itself is a most (if not *the* most) important function in the sense that the form of the environment responds to it. This helps explain why wants are often more important than needs and why apparently 'irrational' choices are made by users. This helps clarify the cases of North Africa, the Motilone, and the Australian aborigines discussed in the introduction. It also plays a major role in helping to explain the major differences in evaluation and preference, and thus choices between users as a whole, and designers, and among different groups of users in any one country or city. More generally, as already discussed, it helps to explain the otherwise puzzling large number of different built environments, such as dwellings.

Variability of norms and standards

In addition to the latent aspect of activities, the various expressions and components of 'culture,' to be discussed in Chapter 7, also play a role in generating environmental variability. One is the variability of norms, and hence of standards. For example, in some work I did with a colleague in the late 1960s, we found that anthropometric standards vary cross-culturally based not only on stature but on how activities are carried out. Major differences were found in stair design (riser/tread relation), storage, recommended temperatures, both generally and for specific rooms, acoustic standards, and lighting standards. Recommended lighting standards for the most difficult seeing tasks were 10 to 20 times higher in the U.S. than in Sweden, Finland, or Switzerland, all highly developed, technologically advanced countries.[10] Similarly, what is considered an acceptable housing density in Hong Kong is about 40-50 times higher than in the United States. Significant differences are also found between the U.S. and Western Europe, and this also applies to the minimum amount of space required per person. It follows that 'high density' in one cultural context can mean something completely different in another. Since 'crowding' is the negative evaluation of particular densities (and some densities may be evaluated as too low), both at the site level and within dwellings, 'culture' plays a significant role in definition of density and space standards.

Culture can play that role in different ways and through different mechanisms. Among these are definitions of desired interactions versus undesired ones, for example, among kin or strangers. The definition of kin also varies cross-culturally. Also variable are the defenses used to cope, which can be physical elements, organization of activities in time, manners and rules regarding interaction, hence privacy mechanisms, and others. We have already seen that the specific systems of settings used greatly change what is considered to be crowded (see Figure 7, p. 22).

The negative effects of density and crowding occur because such situations lead to stress. In this connection, 'culture' needs to be considered in two respects. First, most models of stress include two elements: situations and individuals.

However, stress is the outcome of an evaluation, or matching, of a situation against certain norms, desired levels, the meaning of the situation, etc., and one is dealing with *perceived stress*. For example, the view that density and crowding (itself the result of a negative evaluation of den-

FIGURE 17A. The commonly used two-element model of stress (based on Rapoport A (1978) Culture and the subjective effects of stress. *Urban Ecology* 3(3):244, Fig. 1.).

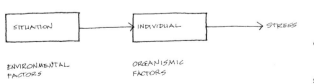

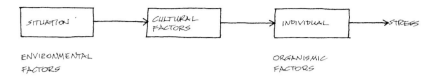

ENVIRONMENTAL
FACTORS

ORGANISMIC
FACTORS

FIGURE 17B.
Three-element
model of stress
(based on *op.cit.*, p.
249, Fig. 3.).

sity) lead to stress due to exposure to strangers depends on who are defined as "strangers," as well as the defenses available. The stressor is then subjectively defined and depends on some norms, expectations, schemata, etc. These, as we will see, are aspects of culture. Therefore, one needs to use a three-element model of stress, which considers the role of culture.

The second way in which culture plays a role in considerations of stress is through the variability of what are considered to be stress-relieving settings (what have been called "restorative environments").[11] Although the literature has emphasized natural environments, and they do seem important, in reality a wide range of settings and behaviors are used, which vary with culture. This variation is found among individuals based on their lifestyle (see Chapter 7) and groups within countries. Some of the mechanisms used, and the related settings, may vary significantly, although I am not aware of research on this topic. Here also, the nature of the system of settings needs to be considered. In cases where all the settings in the system are stressful (including the dwelling), i.e., there are no stress-relieving settings, the problem is far more serious. In any case, the relationship between the primary setting (the dwelling) and the other settings used (in culture-specific ways) within the larger system must always be considered.

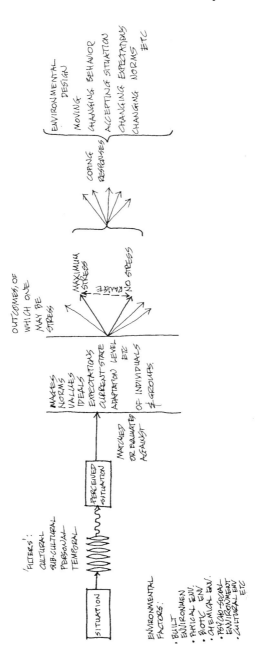

FIGURE 18. A more detailed version of the three-element model in Figure 17B (based on *op.cit.*, p. 246, Fig. 2.).

CHAPTER 4

Preference, Choice, and Design

We have seen that housing, neighborhoods, and other environments are different or are used differently by different groups. There are also cases where one finds evidence of attempts to make environments different (modification and transformations, especially in developing countries where enforcement of codes is often weak). The reason is that such environments need to be supportive for the various groups, to be congruent with their 'culture.' This means that one size does *not* fit everyone as the modern movement thought and most designers still assume implicitly. That means that if there is a choice, i.e., constraints do not dominate, different environments are preferred (or they wouldn't have come into being) or would be preferred. In this connection, it is useful to use the conceptualization of the built environment as cultural landscapes, partly because they include all the scales discussed earlier.

Landscapes express shared preferences
An even more important reason for the utility of this concept in the context of culture-environment relations is that such landscapes are not 'designed' in the usual sense of the word.[12] They are the outcome of many individual decisions of numerous people over long periods of time. The question then becomes how one can explain the systematic, and hence recognizable, nature of such landscapes. The remarkable fact is that if one knows the cues, cultural landscapes are remarkably easy to identify. In fact, often a single glance at an image is sufficient. It seems to me that the only, or at least most likely, explanation is that such landscapes express the preferences shared by groups based on shared ideals, images, and the like expressed in schemata (see Chapter 7). These then guide the choices made so that the apparently independent actions of many people over long time periods add up to a recognizable whole.

As I will shortly elaborate, this consistent application of a particular system of rules for making choices among the alternatives available (or perceived as being available) not only leads to cultural landscapes, including vernacular, but also defines 'design' as it is more commonly understood.

In fact, what is called 'style' in art, environmental design, and other fields is the outcome of just such a process of making choices. Such systematic choices in architecture lead to the styles of ancient Egypt, Greece, Rome, Romanesque vs. Gothic, Renaissance vs. Baroque, and so on. Choice also leads to migration at all scales from international to regional, urban to intraurban, i.e., the neighborhood and dwelling chosen. Like design, migration responds to negative and positive evaluation, the so-called 'pushes' and 'pulls' already discussed. Underlying all these, I suggest, is a single process that can be illustrated as follows (and which, as we have already seen, is also relevant to stress).

FIGURE 19. Model of evaluation process, which, with minor modifications, can be applied to many situations (see Figure 18)

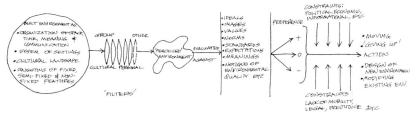

The 'filters' express the fact that one is always dealing with 'perceived' environments and their attributes. Group 'filters' are the result of enculturation at the largest scale, a culture region (Western Europe or North America) or country (Spain or the United States). Subgroups are discussed in Chapter 6; there are usually many, and more specific enculturation or acculturation leads to a variety of 'filters.' Individual 'filters' reflect the results of personal experiences, and the effects can be identified through what have been called "residential histories" or "environmental autobiographies" describing the environments one has lived in, experienced, those most memorable, etc. Individual variety tends to be much greater today than in traditional societies, but cannot play a role in research or design except in the case of the single family house, although even there conflicts and negotiations among family members often occur as a result of their various experiences. There may also be 'filters' resulting from what have been called 'cohort effects,' commonalities among aggregations of individuals due to, for example, being born at a given time.

(based on Rapoport A (2000) Science, explanatory theory, and environment-behavior studies. In S Wapner, *et al.* (Eds.), Theoretical-perspectives in environment-behavior research. New York: Kluwer/Plenum, Fig. 3, p. 131, and Rapoport A (2000) Theory, culture, and housing. *Housing, Theory and Society* 17(4):146, Fig. 1.).

Examples in the U.S. are 'baby boomers' or 'Generation X.' All of these differences not only influence the nature of the 'perceived environment' but also the nature of the ideals, images, schemata, norms, etc., against which the perceived environments are evaluated.[13]

In effect, when people choose an environment, such as housing, they choose not only the particular system of settings and its larger context (discussed earlier) but also the particular environmental quality of those systems (to be discussed shortly) in a particular location, making various tradeoffs between travel time and dwelling size or type, neighborhood vs. dwelling quality, the *social* characteristics of neighbors, and so on. If at all possible, they also frequently modify that environment in various ways, most often by manipulating semi-fixed elements ('personalization'). They do, however, also change fixed-feature elements, if that is not too difficult or expensive, with important implications for the need for open-ended design (to be discussed later). It should also be reiterated that *wants* often play a much more important role than *needs* in preference and choice (including the choices made in design), and that wants are closely related to meaning, and hence to 'culture.' This is clear if one examines advertisements related to housing, which emphasize meanings, and quite frequently do not even show the dwelling but vegetation, views, butterflies, sunsets, human relationships, recreation, and so on.[14]

For example, at this time in the U.S., the size of houses is going up significantly as family size is decreasing. The detached house and its location in a particular landscape, called suburban, are also wants rather than needs. These landscapes themselves vary with culture and change as culture changes. For example, in large areas of Latin America there has been a reversal of what is regarded as a desirable residential environment (see Figure 20, p. 55).

In effect, an environment previously evaluated negatively because it was considered 'disordered' is now evaluated positively; there has been a reversal. I have suggested elsewhere that this is due to a widespread acceptance of the (mainly U.S.) suburban image. These two orders, which result from choices based on values, ideals, images, etc. (i.e., wants), can be described as a geometric order (often

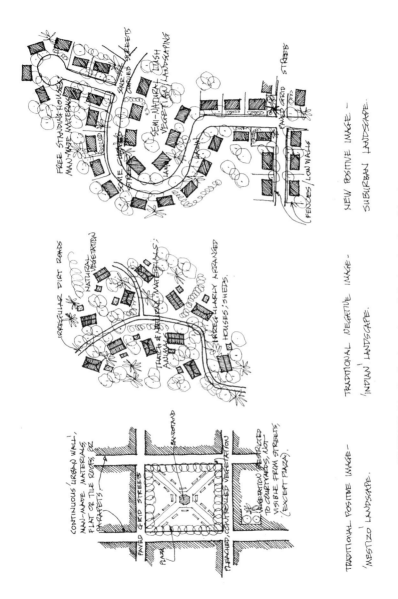

FIGURE 20. Latin-American (Mexican) cultural landscapes

(based partly on Rapoport A (1990) *The meaning of the built environment.* Tucson: University of Arizona Press, Fig. 23, p.146.).

FIGURE 21.
Social vs.
geometric order
(based partly on
op.cit., Fig. 25, p.
149.).

found in Western countries and elite areas in Latin America) as opposed to a social order as found, for example, in pre-contact Africa and North America.

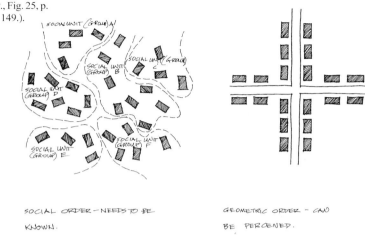

SOCIAL ORDER — NEEDS TO BE KNOWN.

GEOMETRIC ORDER — CAN BE PERCEIVED.

The latter is often misunderstood by members of other groups who see it as representing a lack of order or as being disorderly or chaotic. This is impossible since all environments reflect culture, being cultural landscapes, and culture is orderly, being a system, and leads to the systematic choices that result in cultural landscapes. More generally, one finds members of particular groups describing environments as chaotic when they cannot understand the order, do not like it, or find it unsuitable. Examples include French authors describing U.S. cities as chaotic, U.S. authors similarly describing Islamic cities, and designers and planners describing various environments (roadside strips, spontaneous settlements, etc.) as chaotic. Such differences in preference for different orders can still be found, as will be discussed later in Chapter 6. An order may even be selected, which will be seen as a disorder by other groups, to communicate a particular meaning or message, as in the case of a counter-culture group in California.[15]

Related are evaluations of certain arrangements and space use as 'slums,' and the use of certain materials can also define areas as slums. In one case, the use in the U.S. of plastic brickwork led architects to condemn an area. More generally, one finds an unselfconscious negative evaluation of traditional materials (adobe, mud bricks, thatch) and traditional forms. All represent meanings intimately related to culture, and hence evaluations, preferences, and choices (i.e., wants rather than 'needs').

Environmental Quality

Before turning to the role of choice in design, the issue of evaluation and preference needs to be discussed, clarified, and made more usable. The many characteristics or attributes of environments that respond to wants and are preferred (chosen) or rejected together constitute *environmental quality*, and positive environmental quality ('better' environments) is the goal of all design. It is linked to 'culture' through the need to ask: What is better? Better for whom? How do we know it is better? and so on. It also becomes important to understand what is meant by 'environmental quality' (i.e., to define it), and it is important to make it operational so that it can be studied, analyzed, compared, specified, etc. (i.e., *used).*

Note that there are at least two major meanings, or interpretations, of this concept. One is related to phenomena such as air and water quality, consequences of overpopulation, radiation, thermal and noise pollution, and the like. They are what one could call the physical-chemical-ecological qualities of the environment and are those emphasized by 'environmentalists' and various environmental protection agencies. The second meaning, which is the one with which this book is mainly concerned, is the more variable qualities of environments, which when positive, provide satisfaction to people and which they then choose, rejecting environments with negative attributes. These are the psychological, bio-social, and cultural qualities of environments. Although EBS has mainly been concerned with the latter, the two aspects of environmental quality interact; designers are (or should be) concerned with both, and attempts are being made to link them by including components of both in the same environmental quality profiles. In making "better" environments, the two meanings of environmental quality need to be combined, and designers need to manipulate both.

Two interpretations of environmental quality

Chapter 4

Four aspects of attributes of environmental quality profiles These attributes, or components, of environmental quality can be identified (through dismantling), studied, listed, ranked, and communicated. They are best described and most easily communicated by an *environmental quality profile*. Four aspects of these attributes can vary:

The *nature* of the components showing which components are included or excluded.

FIGURE 22.
Environmental quality profile — variation among components
(based on Rapoport A (1995) Environmental quality and environmental quality profiles. In A Rapoport (Ed.), *Thirty-three papers in environment-behavior research.* Newcastle, U.K.: Urban International Press, Fig. 1, p. 481.).

The *ranking* of these components, i.e., the *relative* importance of the same components.

FIGURE 23.
Environmental quality profile — variation in ranking of same components
(based on *op.cit.*, Fig.2, p. 481.).

58

The *'absolute' importance,* or magnitude, of these components vis-à-vis other things that are not aspects of environmental quality but affect quality of life and, therefore, play a role in *choice.* Recall that I emphasize choice as the most important aspect of the effect of environment on people (basic question 2). Thus, people may deliberately choose worse environmental quality in favor of factors such as income, education, their children's future, etc. This is common in developing countries with regard to urbanization. Thus, for example, and surprisingly, the pavement dwellers of Calcutta have been shown in several studies not to be as dissatisfied as one would expect. They see their children as having the possibility of becoming urbanized. In a study in Jogjakarta, Indonesia, rural immigrants in spontaneous settlements attached *no* importance to environmental quality. After 15 years, and having become part of the formal economy, environmental quality became most important. It is this phenomenon that led Peter Lloyd to ask whether spontaneous settlements in developing countries were 'slums of hope,' as opposed to the objectively higher standards of the 'slums of despair' in developed countries.

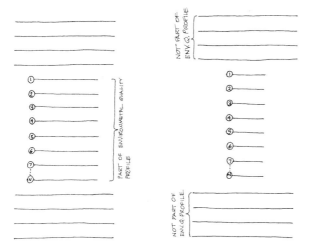

FIGURE 24. Environmental quality profiles — variation in importance vis-à-vis other aspects of life (based on *op.cit.*, Fig. 3, p. 481.).

The components can be *positive* or *negative*. These are the pulls and pushes respectively of migration, or habitat selection, the attributes liked/disliked, sought or avoided/rejected.

FIGURE 25.
Environmental quality profiles — components can be positive or negative (based on *op.cit.*, Fig. 4, p. 482.).

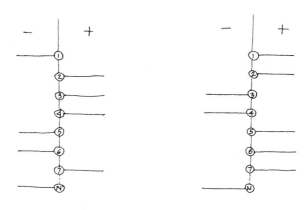

FIGURE 26.
Environmental quality profiles of particular environments. These can also be drawn radially

These four can be combined, allowing the graphic representation in the form of a profile of any particular example of environmental quality.

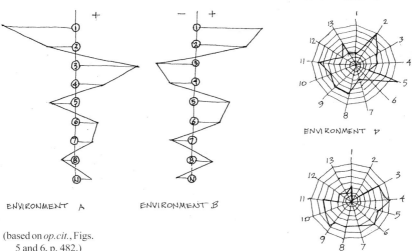

(based on *op.cit.*, Figs. 5 and 6, p. 482.)
(see Khattab O (1993) Environmental quality assessment: An attempt to evaluate government housing projects. *Open House International* 18(4):41-47.).

The components referred to in the figures are only examples. One is dealing with *classes* of components. The specifics can change, components can be added or subtracted, rankings changed, and so on. Conceptually, the general components are more useful because they are likely to be more invariant than the specifics, whatever these might be at a given time and place; they can then be 'plugged in.'

This formulation and the evaluation/choice model (see Figure 19, p. 53) are general, applicable to all situations and at many scales. This has the advantage of linking the large literature on international, interregional, and interurban migration to intraurban habitat selection — the choice of neighborhood, block, lot, and dwelling. This also relates to the earlier discussion of housing as a system of settings embedded in larger systems. What is chosen is a particular system of settings and its associated environmental quality profile; this results in a particular ambience. This is the sum-total of the multisensory experience of the perceptual aspects of the environment. This is commonly called 'aesthetics,' which when considered not just visually but as involving all sense modalities, is more usefully identified as ambience.[16]

This bundle of attributes that makes up environmental quality is the *link between choice and the specifics of particular environments* of all kinds and at all scales. Components of all aspects of environmental quality can be represented, studied, and ranked — locational, physical (climate, topography, views, vegetation, water, noise, pollution, etc.), social (homogeneity, status, family structure, etc.), perceptual (e.g., ambience), cultural (discussed in detail in Chapter 6), concerning meaning (latent aspects, symbolism), and so on. An important characteristic of profiles is their ability to help organize and condense large amounts of information and many diverse *specific* variables, including both the physical/chemical/ecological and psychological/bio-social/cultural. This is largely due to the fact that such profiles can be drawn, i.e., represented graphically. Note also that such profiles are open-ended and allow new data to be introduced. These can be new research findings, changes over time due to culture change, cross-cultural variations among groups, and so on.

The link between choice and specifics

Since much EBS research deals with evaluation and preference, and hence environmental quality, and all design has as its purpose the improvement of environmental quality, the use of profiles allows the integration of much of the research literature; it can be integrated and synthesized, represented and studied by using profiles. It is also very useful in post-occupancy evaluation because it allows one to describe negative, as well as positive, environmental quality, what is disliked and rejected, as well as what is liked and chosen.

Chapter 4

I have already discussed the extraordinary variety of environments and suggested that it is due to latent aspects, i.e., wants. These reflect both positive and negative evaluations of components of environmental quality by their designers (in the broad sense described earlier). They also reflect the role of constraints (to be discussed later). Profiles can then describe and make possible the comparison of the environmental quality of different types of environments: sacred vs. secular, traditional vs. contemporary, high-style vs. vernacular or popular, and so on.

Use of profiles

Although the environmental quality profile is analytically (etic) developed by the researcher, one is concerned with its specifics, i.e., 'perceived' environmental quality of users (emic). These evaluations tend not to be analytical. People react to environments globally and affectively, in terms of "I like it/I do not like it" (although that rationale should not be used by designers!). The analysis is the researchers'. This is why housing 'games,' which also include neighborhoods, work. In them, given choices among alternatives, people are able to quickly and easily make such choices so that their ideals are reflected. When monetary limits are imposed and constrain choice, the order in which various components of environmental quality are eliminated provides a ranking of their importance, from least to most important, from the 'periphery' to their 'core.'

FIGURE 27.
Hypothetical environmental quality profiles of different actors for the same environment
(based partly on Rapoport A (1983) Development, culture, and supportive design. *Habitat International* 7(5/6):263, Fig. 9.).

Because profiles are able to analyze users', designers', and others' preferences, their use also makes possible the identification and comparison of the profiles of different groups. This is particularly important in the context of this book, which deals with 'cultural' (i.e., group) differences and also, of course, similarities. The basic process involves identifying the environmental quality profiles of various actors in the design process, and thus identifying disagreements, areas of conflict, and so on.

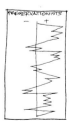 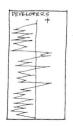 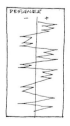 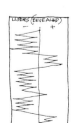 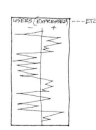

Many examples are possible, and it is relatively easy to do such analyses, and to interpret a large body of research in these terms. I will give just a few, both hypothetical and actual. Thus, considering spontaneous ('squatter') settlements synchronically, one can identify the different profiles of international agencies (for example, negative), designers (Romantic profile), and users (both revealed and expressed profiles). Diachronically over time, one can study changes in such profiles so that the highly negative evaluations of spontaneous settlements by various agencies have become highly positive (excessively so according to some critics).

In the case of Elizabeth New Town, in South Australia, the ranking of the importance of four recreational activities — socializing, semi-socializing activities, sport, and specialized activities — was different among planners and teenagers, i.e., the provision did not match preferences. Three of the four were incongruent (to varying extents, with one reversed) and only one was a match. The verbal display I used in 1977 is more effectively shown as two profiles. Moreover, one could identify preferences for additional activities, differences among sub-groups of teenagers, and changes over time since the new town was built. In the case of another new town, Milton Keynes in the U.K., critics suggested major changes on the basis of negative evaluations of a number of attributes. Among them: difficulties in way-finding by visitors, the lack of 'urbanity,' and the isolation and village-like quality of the neighborhoods. Fortunately, research was done before making any changes. Users agreed about the attributes of the city *but saw them as highly positive.*[17] In effect, these components of the profile were uniformly positive for users and negative for designers and planners.

Major differences in evaluations by designers and users as a whole, although there are numerous differences among groups of users (see Chapter 7), have been identified in the research literature. These can usefully be described by profiles. In one case, Maiden Lane, a housing project in London, won architectural awards and was greatly praised in *The Architectural Review*. In a research study, tenants evaluated it extremely negatively, comparing it to a concentration camp.[18] The components of the positive and negative evaluations are also completely different; there is a complete mismatch between the two. There have also been studies about the very different evaluations of competition entries by a professional jury and the public.[19]

Many other examples can be found of group differences between designers and users, among different groups of users, insiders' vs. outsiders' views about neighborhoods, cross-cultural differences, and changes over time in evaluations in a single culture. All can be described by means of environmental quality profiles and compared, as suggested in Figure 27 on p. 62. In fact, it might even be possible to define groups in terms of their environmental quality profiles.

Using profiles in design   Environmental quality profiles are useful not only in research, they are also useful in design. This is because they make it possible to describe, indeed, to *specify,* the positive and negative attributes of the environment to be designed. In other words, profiles enable one to deal with the critical design questions of *what* to do (and *why*), the rationale which is programming; the question of *how* is then a consideration of ways to reach the desired state and the means available. Evaluation then becomes a way of finding out if one has, in fact, achieved the goal and to what extent. In that connection, one begins to consider various constraints (e.g., of affordability), and here also, profiles can help in leaving out components of environmental quality and would clearly begin with those ranked lowest — reflecting group ('cultural') differences in evaluation and preference.

Design

It may seem strange that in a book dealing with design, I have discussed in some detail people's preferences and choices often in terms of migration and buying or renting housing. But this is linked to design in two ways. First, users rarely get to design their environments, unlike in most preliterate and vernacular situations. Typically they move into or use already existing environments, at best personalizing them by means of semi-fixed elements.[20] But I have suggested that *design is for users*. Therefore, designers are surrogates for users, doing what the latter cannot, or do not wish, to do. Users' preferences are paramount, and the choices users make are the best way to identify revealed preferences; other research identifies expressed preferences (see the two right-hand profiles in Figure 27, p. 62). There is, however, a second and more fundamental reason to approach design in this way. This is that *design itself can be seen as a process of choosing among alternatives*. In this sense, as when users choose habitats, design also involves tradeoffs, i.e., ranking components of environmental quality.

This means that design can be visualized as what I call *the choice model of design*. This heuristic model applies to all types of design, in the sense of any modification of the physical environment — traditional and contemporary, tribal, vernacular, and high-style. It applies to the creation of cultural landscapes (as discussed earlier). It also applies to what students do in studio, or designers in offices; they generate many alternatives, eliminate most using various criteria (which are often as subjective as "I don't like this," although that is unfortunate), and finish up with one which is then drawn-up and presented. In the case of practice, it is built. In all these cases, the important question (usually not sufficiently considered) is what to do and why; how comes later. What varies in all these different kinds of design are the alternatives considered, who makes the choices, over how long a period of time, the criteria used in eliminating alternatives, the ideal model one is trying to reach (however imperfectly), and the rules used in applying the criteria. We have already seen that rules apply in both the creation of cultural landscapes and how settings are used, for what, by whom, when, etc. Recall the general question: Who does what, where, when, including/excluding whom, and why? Rules thus link behavior and design.

Choice model of design

Most of these and other aspects of this model of design are closely related to 'culture.' This will become clearer if I now develop this model step by step beginning with the alternatives considered; these are constrained and defined by culture.

Considering alternatives in the choice model of design

Consider a few examples. There was once a full page advertisement by an environmental organization showing an aerial view of Central Park in New York City as a parking lot covered by cars. I had a slide made and showed it in lectures at various schools of architecture. It was always greeted with uneasy, almost embarrassed laughter. The rea-

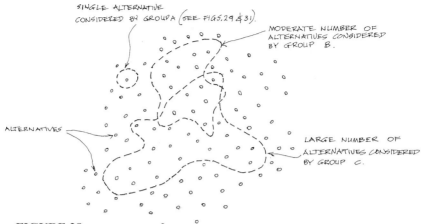

FIGURE 28.
Cultural constraints on alternatives among which choices are made. See Figs. 32 and 33 on pp. 68 and 70.

son, I would suggest, is that no architect, landscape architect, or planner could conceive of this as a viable alternative. When one considers the traditional dwellings of the Pueblo Indians and Navaho in the Southwestern United States, they are very different indeed, although the geographic setting is the same and the two groups have been in contact for a very long time (they are clearly expressions of 'culture').[21] In the case of Pueblos, the choices are among various forms of *clustered* dwellings; among the Navaho, the pattern is of *scattered* dwellings separated by considerable distances.

This is also the case with hospitals, office buildings, supermarkets, and other 'building types.' In all these cases, there is an implicit, unexamined schema that is the starting point of design. It is important to identify, examine, and make it explicit because it is typically highly constrained by cultural presuppositions that may not be appropriate in other cultural contexts, often because of the latent aspects of functions and activities.

FIGURE 29.
The single traditional alternative considered by each of two groups.

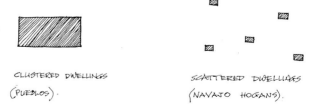

CLUSTERED DWELLINGS
(PUEBLOS).

SCATTERED DWELLINGS
(NAVAJO HOGANS).

With the 'what' predetermined as it were, choices are made regarding shape or materials (the 'how').

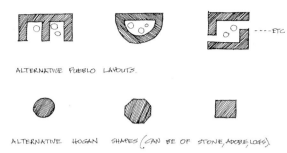

ALTERNATIVE PUEBLO LAYOUTS.

ALTERNATIVE HOGAN SHAPES (CAN BE OF STONE, ADOBE, LOGS).

FIGURE 30.
Variations resulting from choices made within a single basic alternative.

In the case of some areas (e.g., the Middle East), it is 'known' that the dwelling in traditional situations would face inwards, be a courtyard-house; in Western Europe it would be outward facing. The choices are about size, shape, materials, etc.[22]

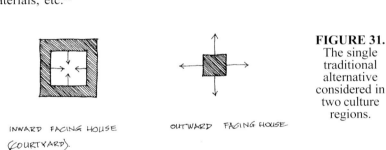

INWARD FACING HOUSE
(COURTYARD).

OUTWARD FACING HOUSE

FIGURE 31.
The single traditional alternative considered in two culture regions.

It is important to note that the basic decision is almost pre-determined: The group shares a single model (the set of alternatives is effectively one), which is then an important part of its culture and sometimes even a symbol of identity — some nomads in central Asia are known as "the people of the black tent" — and most traditional groups can be identified with a dwelling (as well as dress, food, and many other aspects of material culture). This is different at present where the initial set of alternatives is extensive. Also, the means available — materials, technology, environmental controls — are limited in most traditional situations and very extensive today (within affordability constraints). This change over historical time is most significant in studying and understanding environments, and can be seen happening very fast in developing countries. It is an aspect of 'modernization' or 'westernization,' better understood as an aspect of *culture change.*[23]

Eliminating alternatives

Alternatives are eliminated from the set 'available' (i.e., considered) by applying various choice criteria. These reflect images, schemata, etc., expressing the ideals of groups, i.e., the notion of ideal people living ideal lives in ideal environments. Through successive elimination, one alternative remains as the final choice.

FIGURE 32. Choice criteria (A, B, C, ... , N) used to eliminate alternatives resulting in one — the "choice model of design" (based in part on Rapoport A (1977) *Human aspects of urban form.* Oxford: Pergamon, Fig. 1.7, p. 17.).

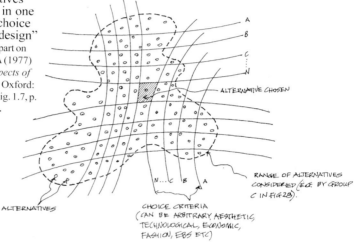

Who applies the choice criteria?

Who applies the criteria (i.e., designs) is a function of the cultural system. In traditional societies (especially tribal and preliterate societies), they may be the users themselves, either men or women (or both), depending on the group. In some cases, men and women are responsible for different aspects and components of buildings. In peasant societies they may be part-time specialists, or they may be full-time specialists. Both may co-exist in the same group so that, as in parts of Oceania, houses may be built by users whereas chiefs' and canoe houses, which have ritual connotations, may be built by specialists; this is also the case in Northern Nigeria where, unlike houses, religious buildings (mosques) are built by specialists, and in the Sepik River area of Papua/New Guinea where men's houses (*haus tambaran*), unlike other structures, involve specialists. Similar differences still persist, although users rarely design, except in developing countries. Unlike 'popular' en-

vironments, high-style buildings are designed by specialist professional designers (architects) or as is increasingly
the case, especially for major buildings and projects, by
large teams of specialist professionals. In all these cases,
one can expect that the different 'actors' will use different
criteria and make different choices, reflecting different preferences based on different ideals, images, and schemata
leading to different environmental quality profiles.

The time over which the choice criteria are applied also
varies greatly with 'culture.' In pre-literate/tribal and vernacular design, the process is *selectionist*, i.e., evolutionary: the environment gradually changing as successive
choices are made. This progressively makes the environment more congruent with users, more supportive. The time
scale is rather long. In such cases, it has generally been
held that the rules behind the criteria involved in the choice
process are usually implicit, informal, and unwritten. (This
is, of course, the case in the creation of cultural landscapes,
as discussed earlier.) Although generally the case, there
are, however, instances where the rules in vernacular design are written and explicit, although even in the best
documented case they are modified by informal, traditional
rules.[24] Although there has been little research on such
rule systems, it seems possible to identify such rules.[25]

Selectionist process of design

In professional design today, the process is *instructionist:*
experts on the large teams involved produce sets of instructions — drawings, specifications, or models — for other
expert teams to execute, and the time-scale is rather short.
There are many formal, explicit, written, legalistic, and
legally enforceable rules — zoning, setbacks, site coverage, health, safety, fire, union, lending agency, insurance,
aesthetic, and many others — that greatly constrain design. They are, in effect, a set of choice criteria not under
designers' control, and they become major determinants
of built environments. Identifying such differences among
rule systems is very useful in identifying characteristics of
different forms of design.

Instructionist process of design

In more general terms, the criteria used in the choice process of design are of many kinds. They may be religious,
as in many tribal, vernacular, and traditional contexts;
without considering them, many traditional environments
cannot be understood. Although they generally weaken and
disappear with 'modernization,' they may persist in cer-

Different cultures use different criteria

tain 'cultures' and even spread into new ones, as is currently the case with the Chinese system of Feng Shui. Criteria may be pragmatic, for example, instrumental (protection from animals, other people, climate), technological, aesthetic, economic, based on EBS research, status oriented, and so on. Different 'cultures' tend to use, or emphasize, different criteria, since typically many are used. The criteria used, their ranking, the underlying schemata, and ideals and rules systems in many cases can be used to identify and understand cultural differences among groups and environments; they help explain how different environments come to be (process).

Different criteria lead to different results

Different criteria lead to different results, for example, the subjective aesthetic criteria of high-style architects vs. the economic criteria of developers or EBS-based culturally-specific criteria. But even when the same or similar criteria are applied, their ranking or order of application makes a major difference. Assume for simplicity that only three criteria are being used: A — economic, B — technological, and C — EBS-based. Which criterion is applied first defines the search-space to which subsequent criteria are applied and subsequent choices made. Yet these subsequent criteria may require choices to be made in a totally different part of the search space. Since the first choice precludes those, it is, therefore, critical.

FIGURE 33.
Importance of the order of application of various choice criteria.

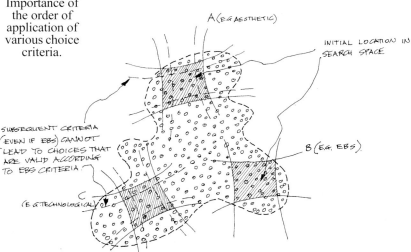

Consider two examples. In the design of housing for Navaho, it has been shown that modern houses are desired (preferred, wanted). Hogans, which are still important in connection with ceremonies and rituals, can be built if and when needed. The settlement pattern, however, remains most important.[26] That pattern can be represented thus:

FIGURE 34.
House layout according to 'cultural' and social criteria (services to be designed accordingly).

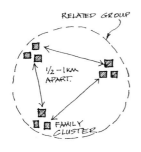
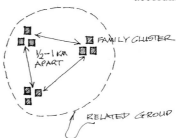

Once such an EBS-based (in this case 'cultural') criterion is applied, the layout of services and infrastructure, such as access, water, waste, and electricity need to be decided upon, i.e., technological and economic criteria applied. Such criteria then become constraints rather than determinants. These may then demand different, often highly innovative technologies very different from those commonly used (roads, gutters, waterpipes, sewers, and the like). The importance of such services vis-à-vis lot size, spacing, social networks, etc. may also vary, i.e., their importance as part of environmental quality needs criteria are applied first, then roads, pipes, and wires determine the layout, which is not supportive of culture-specific needs.

FIGURE 35.
House layout based on services layout, e.g., sewers. 'Culturally' and socially appropriate house layout is impossible.

Even if one then tries to allocate houses to related groups on the basis of EBS knowledge (which is not usually done), the results may be, and have often been, highly unsatisfactory.

Certain other decisions at the scale of project location, cluster or neighborhood definition, lot size and shape, circulation patterns, open space distribution, as well as the location of services discussed above, may block important relationships. For example, in developing countries it is often the case that self-built dwellings tend to provide culturally-valid settings and spatial organization. If, however, the above larger-scale decisions based on non-EBS criteria are inappropriate, such appropriate organization may become difficult or impossible to achieve. For example, if the required organization is of a compound type, i.e., a group of dwelling elements sharing a more or less common private space, then a layout based on individual lots arranged along linear roads will make such an organization impossible.[27]

FIGURE 36. Different layouts and their corresponding land subdivisions.

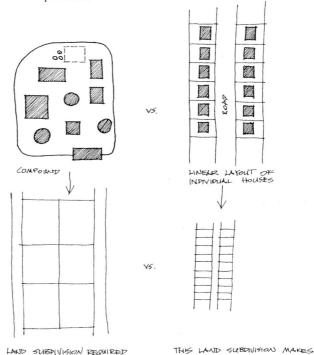

Meaning plays important role in environmental quality

It is clear, even from this brief discussion, that the criteria used and how they are applied reflect some ideal, some notion of ideal people leading ideal lives in ideal environments. These are embodied in images and schemata, often (or *usually*) unarticulated, beyond awareness, and implicit, although research can identify them. These in turn (as will be seen in Chapter 6) are linked to norms, standards, etc. All of these, through the choices made, lead to particular notions of environmental quality. Given the importance of latent aspects, meaning plays an important role, so that environmental quality is intimately related to status, identity, etc. The rules used to apply the choice criteria are, as already suggested several times, 'cultural,' and once again, groups ('cultures') can be defined at least partly by their rules, schemata, and ideals.

As cultures change, so do the ideals and images. They may become more different, for example, to reinforce group identity, changing ideologies in the response known as 'defensive structuring'[28] — a response to cultural and social stress — and other reasons. However, as 'cultures' change, they may begin to converge to common ideals, images, and consequently, environments. A particularly striking current example is the spread of what one could term the 'suburban image': detached single-family dwellings at relatively low perceived densities with much vegetation and greenery and, with other uses, segregated.[29] This is happening all over the world — examples can be found in Thailand, Russia, Turkey, Italy, France, many African countries, and Latin America. In fact, it is difficult to find places where suburbanization is not occurring and, as is often the case, this is documented better in the mass media than the research literature.[30] There seems to be a clear tendency for housing to become 'suburban' as soon as resources increase, i.e., when *constraints weaken*. This suggests that such environments reflect wants; they represent choices previously blocked. As in the case of Milton Keynes discussed earlier, there is evidence that some of the characteristics of suburbs criticized by designers and others — anonymity, lack of public spaces, lack of other uses — are those seen as highly positive and desirable by residents.[31] Clearly this is an instance of conflicting environmental quality profiles (see Figure 27, p. 62).

Several examples should help clarify the intimate link between the suburban image, environmental quality, and choice. One is the 'Australian Green Streets Project (New Choices in Housing).' It has been government policy in Australia for some time to encourage 'densification,' although there is some professional opposition. Public oppo-

The suburban image

sition is very strong. Ignoring for the moment the validity of this policy, the intention of the Green Streets Project is to reduce public opposition and to influence the public to accept densification as desirable. One approach has been to use marketing organizations to try and discover, for the relevant government department, which components are acceptable and which are not, e.g., the minimum street width, spacing of dwellings, lot size, and the like. The intention is to retain acceptable attributes and eliminate those that are not acceptable — in my terms, to eliminate negative components of the environmental quality profile. Of particular interest is a series of posters meant to convince the public about the merits of the program. The striking thing about these posters is that they emphasize trees, lawns, plantings, and open space to the extent that buildings tend to recede into the background. The image of these denser developments is clearly that of suburbia and of low perceived density; there is little doubt about the environmental quality profile being communicated.

In Quebec, Canada, the provincial government is funding a research project to identify those modifications to 1950s suburban developments, now becoming obsolescent, that are acceptable to inhabitants, i.e., trying to identify their environmental quality profiles to guide policy and design.

Another striking example comes from Mexico (in the case I know, the area near Guadalajara), although it is relevant in large areas of Spanish Latin America. In that tradition, two cultural landscapes are found: one characterizing the mestizo, and hence high-status environment, the other the Indian, hence low-status environment. In the newly developed, prestigious suburban developments, it is effectively the 'Indian' landscape that is the model, although it is clear from the sales literature that the model is really the United States (see Figure 20, p. 55). This Mexican example is particularly telling because, in effect, there is a reversal in the evaluation of the image involved and its corresponding environmental quality profile. It is a result of a new ideal and the corresponding culture change. The highly positive image of the suburban image is also clear from an analysis of new housing developments in Jogjakarta, Indonesia, and around Istanbul, Turkey. In those cases, English names and facilities typical of U.S. developments are also present. It would be interesting and useful to discover whether there are any culture-specific differences in plans, style, color, materials, site layout, etc. No such research exists, as far as I know. The suburban image is certainly not universal, and there are countervailing (although I believe much weaker) trends toward densification, co-housing, communal housing, and downtown living. The best-known reaction is 'traditional neighborhood design,' but it still retains many elements of the suburban image. Moreover, it still forms a very small part of new construction.

A Cautionary Note

Much of the literature on culture-environment relations, including mine, has emphasized the importance of culture and its role in understanding and designing environments. In this chapter I have continued this tradition. But how important culture is vis-à-vis other human characteristics is an empirical question, as is the nature of the situations, when it is important, and for which groups of people. I have already suggested that it is rapid culture change (e.g., developing countries or immigrant populations), threats to identity, and other social, cultural, economic, and other forms of stress. It is then that defensive structuring and supportiveness become especially important in situations that I call high criticality.[32] One also needs to discover empirically the environments for which culture is more or less important. Hypotheses are, however, possible. My assumption in this book is that housing (in the broad sense described) is where culture is most important. It is likely that shopping, which often has major latent functions, is significantly influenced by culture (although possibly not in its image, and hence appearance) in terms of latent functions. There is also evidence of a role for culture in hospitals and clinics, although once again this may be in non-visual aspects, not the visual characteristics emphasized by architects. Attempts to provide culture-specific visual elements in the case of high-rise office buildings have been criticized and seem wrong. That is, I would also argue the case of airports, universities, high-tech industries (biomedical, electronic), and so on. In all those cases there may, of course, be significant non-visual cultural specifics (in privacy, status, penetration gradients, relationships, etc.); I have suggested above that this may even be the case in housing, where a modern image and traditional organization and use may be the preferred solution.

Importance of culture

In all these and other cases, however, empirical research is essential, which is the role of EBS. Scales could be produced, based on research, showing when culture is most important and when it is least important. If such data are not available, these scales could be hypotheses to be tested. In any case, *they are all empirical questions.*

But however important culture is, either generally or in any given case, and despite increasing interest and literature on the subject, 'culture' has been little used in design. As I like to put it, paraphrasing Mark Twain, 'culture' in design is like the weather, "everyone talks about it, but no one does anything about it." Why that is the case is a very important question, and my answers to it are central to this book. I think that there are two major reasons why 'culture' has not been used in design, and these are related.[33] The first is that the nature of the concept of culture has been very unclear and not discussed explicitly. It is, therefore, necessary to review and discuss definitions of culture and clarify which definition(s) might be most useful in environmental research and design. This I do in the next two chapters (5 and 6). The second reason, and the one which I regard as the main conclusion of this book, leads to the suggestion that a new and different approach to 'culture' is needed in order to make it possible to *use* culture in research, programming, design, and evaluation. This is the subject of Chapter 7.

Why is culture rarely used in design?

CHAPTER 5

The Nature of Culture

The first thing to note is that 'culture' is not a 'thing' but an idea, a concept, a *construct:* a label for the many things people think, believe, and do and how they do them. It was, in fact, first proposed and used in its current anthropological sense in 1871 in England by E. B. Tylor, who is often considered to be the first anthropologist. In this sense, the term 'culture' did not appear in English dictionaries, i.e., was not in general use, until the 1920s. In some languages, the concept in its anthropological (or technical) sense is still lacking; it is used, rather, in its more traditional sense of civilization, of being a 'cultured person' in terms of manners, knowing food and wine, music, art, and literature, having 'cultivated taste.' But the anthropological use of the term is spreading.

Definition of culture

Tylor's original 1871 definition was that culture "is the complex whole which includes knowledge, belief, art, law, morals, customs, and any other capabilities and habits acquired by man as a member of society." This is still a useful definition, but it seems clear that it includes (almost) everything that characterizes humans. Since then there have been hundreds of definitions, and by 1952, a 436-page book reviewed the numerous definitions and concepts of culture;[34] this process has continued since. This clearly makes matters difficult and confusing. Fortunately, I believe that it is possible to simplify the problem by identifying and dealing with *types* or *classes* of definitions. It is possible to identify three types (or classes) of definitions that address the question of what culture is and, more recently and therefore less known and with fewer examples, three types (or classes) of definitions that address the question of what culture does, i.e., what it is for. This is a useful approach that is being increasingly used in a number of fields. I will not be dealing with that general question of what culture is for, but that essentially asks why humans should have culture in the first place. It clearly must have had some advantages or it would not have evolved under selection pressures.

Chapter 5

What is culture?

Concerning the question of what culture is, one type of definition describes it as the way of life of a people, including their ideals, norms, rules, routinized behaviors, etc. A second class of definitions defines it as a system of schemata transmitted symbolically across generations, through the enculturation (or socialization) of children and acculturation of immigrants. This transmission occurs not only through language, example, etc. but also through the built environment, the way settings are used. The third type of definition defines culture as a means of ecological adaptations, the use of resources, and the principal attribute that enables humans to make a living by exploiting various eco-systems. Although the correspondence is not as clear as it might seem, one could say that cultural anthropology and ethnography emphasize the way of life of groups, cognitive and symbolic anthropology, the symbolic role of culture, and ecological anthropology, the 'economic' role of culture.

What does culture do?

Concerning the question of what culture does, one can also identify three types of answers, i.e., definitions. The first is that the purpose of culture is to provide a 'design for living' through various rules as to how things should be done. One metaphor then compares it to a blueprint for assembling components, a second to a set of instructions (like DNA), which is more useful because it is dynamic. On the second view, the purpose of culture is to provide the framework that gives meaning to particulars — 'things' only have meaning in relation to each other in some framework. The third type of answer is that the purpose of culture is to define groups: the many groups ('pseudospecies') of which our single biological species is composed. In that sense, its purpose is to separate groups, to make them distinct and different from one another.

The definitions of culture are complementary

It is important to emphasize that these various classes of definitions should not be taken as 'right' or 'wrong.' Rather, different definitions (or conceptualizations) of culture are useful for different concerns (i.e., in different domains or subdomains) and in dealing with various questions. Moreover, these classes of definitions are not conflicting or contradictory, they are *complementary* so that the first three are easily linked among themselves, as well as the second three, and finally all six. For example, culture evolved as a way of making a living, exploiting the resources of eco-systems. That leads to particular ways of doing things, i.e.,

78

a way of life. Through symbolic transmission this way of life is perpetuated across generations. Similarly, the 'design for living' leads to the development of frameworks within which particulars take on meaning. The different frameworks then lead to group differences. Rather than linking all six, I would suggest that readers do it; a useful way is to list them and use arrows to relate them to each other.

It is also most important to emphasize that culture is not 'free,' that there is not complete relativism, which was the usual view in anthropology during most of the 20th century and is still the most dominant. It is, however, starting to change, albeit slowly and with major disagreements and sometimes very heated arguments between those who believe that there are evolutionary biological constraints on culture, and hence universals and 'human nature,' and those who still support the view that culture is 'free' and, therefore, that relativism reigns. It does seem clear, however, that there is a gradually growing realization that biological and evolutionary constraints exist and, as a result, increasing awareness over the past few decades of the existence of human universals, human nature, and hence constancies. The issue is not, however, constancy or difference; both clearly exist and play a role. Once again, it is rather the relative importance (or contribution) of constancy and specificity in various contexts and situations. These should not be assumed *a priori* but should be seen as empirical questions, leading to a more nuanced view with constancy, universals, and human nature, as well as cultural specifics and differences, being recognized and needing to be discovered.

There is no complete relativism

In any case, this is an important issue that one needs to know about, and one needs to keep up with developments and change in the evidence as research continues (and accelerates). It is also important to realize that culture itself has evolved and can be traced back to animal origins through proto-culture(s). How far back it can be traced is still being vigorously debated. There are also some suggestions that with the development of culture in humans, it in turn may have influenced evolution, but this does not concern us here.

The possible existence of universals is, however, important, especially in connection with the concerns of this

Existence of universals

FIGURE 37.
'Culture' as completely variable.

book. This is because it may reduce the extent of variability, making EBS research and design easier. If culture is strictly relative, we have the following situation.

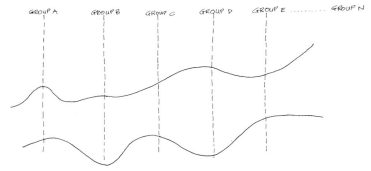

FIGURE 38.
Possible constant and variable aspects of 'culture.'

If, however, there is some constancy, then variability is reduced, the extent of that reduction depending on the degree of constancy.

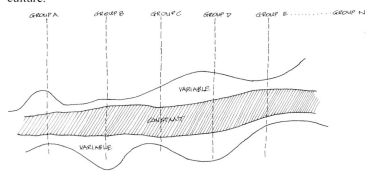

Constancy and change

It also appears increasingly likely that different human phenomena show varying degrees of constancy and also varying rates of change. Thus, it has been suggested that among the most conserved cultural characteristics are family structure, early learning in the family (enculturation), and so on. Perception is more constant than cognition and much more constant than evaluation and preference, although there are constraints and some constancy. Traits that depend on the degree of social evolution (e.g., socio-economic characteristics) do not change rapidly, so that not only the extent of constancy but also the rates of change in any given characteristic need to be discovered. For our purposes it is important to note that *the form and structure of dwellings* also tend not to change rapidly when considered historically; they seem to be accelerating at the moment, and it is the synthesis (or syncretism) between constant, slowly changing elements and rapidly changing elements that is important, as discussed earlier.

There is also a possibility that some apparent similarities are actually differences. Possibly even important is that some apparent variability may in fact be different expressions of constancy.

FIGURE 39. Constant and variable aspects of 'culture,' with the possibility of specific expressions of constants

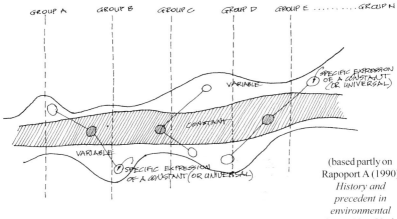

One example is privacy. At first glance, different groups seem to have very different needs for and forms of privacy. However, privacy is, in fact, a human universal in the sense that there is always some avoidance of unwanted interaction, i.e., control of interaction and information flows. What varies is the definition of 'interaction' and 'unwanted' (i.e., between whom and whom, when, where, and why), the different sense modalities emphasized, and the mechanisms involved. These latter include rules and manners, organization of time (temporal), spacing, use of physical elements, psychology (withdrawal), and so on.[35] As a result, what appear to be very different urban fabrics can be shown to be just different ways of controlling unwanted interaction.[36]

(based partly on Rapoport A (1990) *History and precedent in environmental design.* New York: Plenum, Fig. 3.12, p. 111; (1998) Using "culture" in housing design. *Housing and Society* 25(1/2):14, Fig. 7; (2001) Architectural anthropology or environment behavior studies. In MJ Amerlinck (Ed.), *Architectural anthropology.* Westport, CT: Bergin and Garvey, Fig. 2.1, p. 32.).

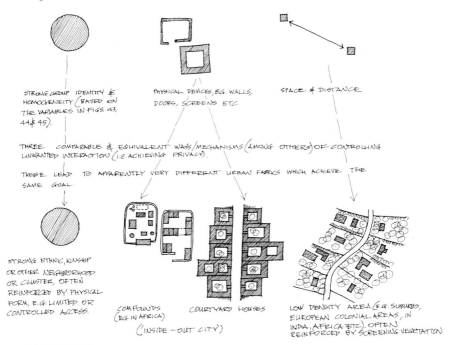

FIGURE 40.
Different specific expressions of a cultural universal — the need to control unwanted interaction, i.e., achieve privacy
(based partly on Rapoport A (1977) *Human aspect of urban form.* Oxford: Pergamon, Fig. 6.1, p. 337, and Fig. 6.2, p. 339, cf. pp. 289-298.).

Finally, it should be noted that whatever the final verdict on these rather theoretical, but important, matters will be regarding the analysis of environments, the design of culture-specific, supportive environments, and the evaluation of how supportive given environments are for various groups, it is generally the *specifics* of the group in question that are most important.

CHAPTER 6

The 'Scale' of Culture

I have already suggested that although an important role of culture is to define groups, the nature of the groups that are relevant in culture-environment relations is a badly under-researched topic in EBS. At issue is the very important question as to the 'scale' at which culture operates, i.e., *the size of relevant groups*. This has generally not been considered, discussed, or researched. Yet in designing for culture, the first step is clearly to identify the number and nature of the relevant groups.

Although there has been no *explicit* discussion of the size of groups, it seems clear that in discussions concerning culture-environment relations, the *implicit* assumption is that groups are large. For example, they are often equated with countries, even large and heterogeneous countries like the U.S., and it is, of course, also the case that in many countries (e.g., Western Europe), the heterogeneity of populations is increasing. In fact, the evidence that I have recently collected suggests that such groups may actually be *rather small.*[37] This relatively small size of groups is a general phenomenon not sufficiently emphasized in discussions of 'culture' or 'society' or in dealing with groups such as 'the elderly,' 'the children,' 'the homeless,' 'the urban poor of the Third World,' etc. These latter, used in EBS, typically comprise numbers of sub-groups, which need to be discovered. The small size of groups means that there are many different groups, as one would suspect given the variety of environments discussed earlier.

Are groups large or small?

In Guatemala, 60% of the approximately 4.5 million inhabitants are Mayan. However, they are divided into 21 different languages, and language is a good indicator of groups since it defines and separates them. The average size of these groups is 130,000; I would add that, in connection with housing, this number can probably be subdivided further by degree of modernization, education, occupation, place of residence (e.g., size and location of settlement), sex, age, etc., further reducing group size. The non-Mayan part of the population with its subdivision would further increase the potential number of groups in this one relatively small country.

In larger countries, the number of groups is larger and there is also more uncertainty about the figures.

Thus, in the case of India in a population of 920 million, it is suggested that there are 4,200 distinct communities, 1,652 dialects, 18 official languages, and 9 major religions; there are also 26 states. Another source refers to 4,635 distinct human communities, such as castes, tribes, and the like. These use 324 functioning languages employing 25 different scripts. Characteristics such as those discussed in the case of Guatemala might well result in many more lifestyle groups that are relevant for design (to be discussed in Chapter 7).

There is also uncertainty regarding Nigeria. There, in addition to the three major groups — Yoruba, Hausa/Fulani, and Ibo — some estimates refer to 250 and others to 300 additional ethnic/tribal groups, i.e., *the actual number is uncertain*. There, as elsewhere in the world, this leads to conflicts. These are particularly severe in the Niger delta where in a small area the grain is extraordinarily fine in the number of groups, their languages, and their spatial arrangements. Once again, when the other attributes I mentioned earlier are considered, the number of groups relevant to physical environments, especially housing, is likely to increase.

This extremely fine grain is also found in Burma (Myanmar). There, in a small area of 20 x 6 km (Nyaung-shwe) in the south of Shan state, are six *minority* groups (i.e., in addition to the majority), which are *not* discussed. These minority groups speak four languages and inhabit very different house and settlement forms. Once again, the number could go up if the variables discussed above are considered. However, it should be pointed out that the contrary process is also possible, that of acculturation/assimilation/modernization, voluntary or forcible. In that case, national and even global patterns may be adopted (as in the case of the suburban image discussed earlier), where global, Western norms, values, and schemata may lead to similar house and settlement forms, materials, etc. Technological and economic forces, as well as policy and politics, may also lead to convergence, i.e., reduce the number of groups relevant for design. On the other hand, the number may increase as 'roots' and ethnicity, and other identities, are sought and re-established and, as a result, new groups may emerge based on the specifics of the processes of syncretism/synthesis. Clearly these phenomena are dynamic and complex and need research to provide empirical data; specifics *need to be discovered not assumed.*

Dynamics apply not only to culture change but to population growth. For example, in Ethiopia the population grew from 25 million in the 1960s to estimates of 60-65 million now. In the 1960s, there were over 70 ethnic groups, many languages, and several religions. Due to political events, the current figures are unknown. On the one hand, the variables already suggested may increase the number of groups. At the same time, however, wars, revolutions, famines, government policies, and modernization may reduce them. The number of relevant groups is difficult to discover. In the adjacent Horn of Africa (Somalia), which is not a huge area, there are over 70 ethnic groups divided into clans and sub-clans, different religions, etc. Some are sedentarized, some nomadic, others yet town dwellers; there are also many refugees. War has greatly complicated matters. Again, it is an empirical question how many groups are relevant in relation to built environments and what continuing changes are most likely.

Increasing heterogeneity

The above examples are all from developing countries partly, as pointed out, because they make useful 'model systems' where conditions and problems are more extreme and, therefore, phenomena are seen more clearly. It might be thought, however, that with continued development and modernization the number of groups inevitably diminishes so that the 'scale' of culture increases. But this is not necessarily so, as the numerous current ethnic 'revivals' and related conflicts show. Also, increasing immigration flows have led to increasing heterogeneity of populations (e.g., in the U.S. and Western Europe), with attendant problems and conflicts often in the news. In Britain due to various waves of migration, there has recently developed a government ethnic housing initiative, which still seems too broad since there are likely to be many more lifestyle groups with varying levels of acculturation and various forms of syncretism. This increase in the number of groups may be temporary, but the time scale is such that design needs to respond. In any case, there is evidence for the large number of groups in developed countries, such as the United States.

According to one study in the U.S., although there seemed to be no socio-economic or regional differences in housing preferences,[38] there were sex and age differences. There has been research on group characteristics relevant to other domains, which may be reflected in environmental preferences. For example, in relation to elections, one political consultant uses 62 'lifestyle clusters' whereas another uses 120 ethnic categories. Also, new fields, such as collaborative conflict management in design and planning, have developed largely in response to the diversity of the U.S. population. The presence of different groups with different values, social roles, etc. leads to conflicts that need to be resolved. For example, recent advertisements for a bond-issue in Miami (bonds are used in the U.S. to finance urban housing, school, and other developments) were tailored to appeal to various groups: ethnic, voter, social change movements, advocacy groups, special interest groups, etc.

In the 1970s in the U.S., four lifestyle groups were being used that were relevant for marketing and housing. Since then, the number has steadily gone up and they are increasingly used, available commercially as lifestyle profiles. One of these uses eight groups, others 43 and 50, respectively. These only include potential buyers of new housing. Considering buyers of existing houses, renters, residents of 'mobile homes,' the homeless, etc., more such groups are likely. Also, in the United States, multiple and overlapping group memberships are typical, further increasing the number of potential groups. The small size of groups is also shown by studies that show the presence of several distinct groups in quite small urban areas. Such groups are defined by geographics, demographics, and psychographics and are used to 'segment' markets. Not only is different housing required for different groups but also different advertisements and sales techniques. Differences among groups in the U.S. also influence marketing more generally and the nature, design, and location of shops, including supermarkets, their location, the goods carried, displays, etc. Recall that shops are part of the housing system of settings.

An additional phenomenon is increasing heterogeneity in Western Europe and the United States. In the latter, there are many hundreds of new immigrant groups. The effects on physical environments are significant. For example, many Chinese immigrants have settled in California, and the traditional geomantic system of Feng Shui is now widely used in the design of housing and office and medical buildings. This has also been found in Canada and the United Kingdom. Newspaper accounts, as well as research, illustrate major impacts of various immigrant groups on environmental design.[39] I will consider just one — 'Hispanics' (or 'Latinos') — which is, of course, far too broad a category.

Immigration increases heterogeneity

One newspaper story concerns an attempt to impose rent controls in Los Angeles. It was expected that Hispanics would support this attempt, since they tend to have low income. However, in a referendum they overwhelmingly voted against it. The reason apparently had to do with kinship relations, the major concern being the ability to retain the possibility of extended family co-residence, which the proposed legislation would have made more difficult. It is important to note that the definition of 'family' also varies among groups. For example, it is defined much more broadly in Mexico than the U.S. and includes what in Anglo-American (and possibly other Western) societies would be considered rather distant kin. This is also the case in traditional China.[40] A related preference seems to play a role in recent findings about the non-use of child-care facilities by this group. The reason given is a "cultural preference for family-like care," so that relatives are preferred. When children are placed in daycare, a family-like model is preferred in which one person watches a number of children in a house. These patterns are the result of a cultural preference to keep children in a warm, family atmosphere based on personal relationships rather than professionalism. There are links here with family structure, social networks, values, lifestyle, and the like.

Differences in housing preferences among groups

For the same group and for similar reasons, this leads to very different preferences regarding the grouping of houses and subdivision layout, as was found in Arizona in a study comparing Anglos and Hispanics.

The two groups also preferred different house styles. In other studies it was found that there are clear differences

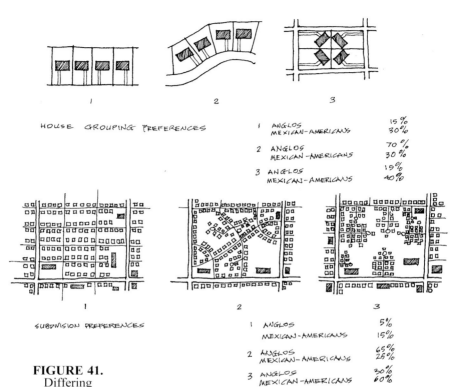

HOUSE GROUPING PREFERENCES

1 ANGLOS		15%
MEXICAN-AMERICANS		30%
2 ANGLOS		70%
MEXICAN-AMERICANS		30%
3 ANGLOS		15%
MEXICAN-AMERICANS		40%

SUBDIVISION PREFERENCES

1 ANGLOS		5%
MEXICAN-AMERICANS		15%
2 ANGLOS		65%
MEXICAN-AMERICANS		25%
3 ANGLOS		30%
MEXICAN-AMERICANS		60%

FIGURE 41.
Differing preferences for house groupings and subdivision layouts, Anglos vs. Mexican-Americans (redrawn from Wheeler L (1977) Behavioral and social aspects of the Santa Cruz Riverpark project. *Man-Environment Systems* 7:203-205.).

in the colors used, landscaping, fences, and decorations among Mexican immigrants and Anglos. When clustering can occur at the neighborhood level, a distinct cultural landscape (or 'housescape') results in communicating identity. That will generally change over time with acculturation.

There may also be highly culture-specific internal treatment of dwellings, as was found for another Hispanic subgroup: Puerto Ricans in Boston. People were found to spend much effort and resources to achieve a highly culture-specific 'aesthetic complex' to communicate group identity. In that case, the dwellings were high-rise apartments and attempts were made, as much as possible, to use space in a manner resembling houses with 'patios' in Puerto Rico, with the living room playing the role of 'patio.'[41] In another study in one area of Arizona and in the same suburban houses, space and room, especially bedroom, use was

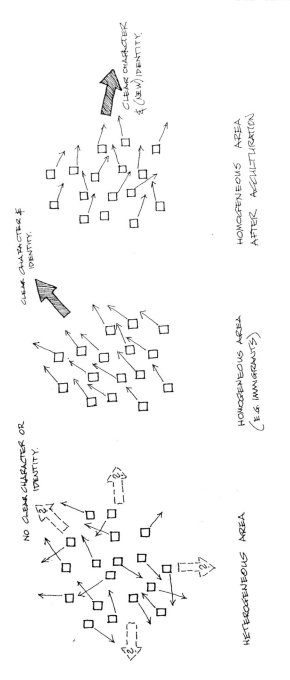

FIGURE 42. Personalization in heterogeneous and homogeneous areas

(based partly on Rapoport A (1990) *The meaning of the built environment*. Tucson: University of Arizona Press, Fig. 21, p. 138.).

quite different for Anglos, Hispanics, and Navaho.[42] As in the case of external colors, decoration, and landscaping among Mexican immigrants, space and room-use patterns also change with acculturation from 'Mexican' to 'American.' This can lead to conflicts between immigrant parents and U.S.-born teenage offspring.

Three conclusions about groups and housing

Even from this brief discussion of one (excessively broad) group and housing, three things follow. The first is that the nature of the dwelling, its size, what it should include, spatial arrangements, style, landscaping, exterior color, exterior and interior décor, etc. can, and will, all vary. Second, at the level of the house-group, and at the neighborhood level, different spatial arrangements will often be wanted. This suggests that the clustering of like people should be made possible or even encouraged. Third, it shows the need for, and hence special provision of, various culture-specific settings and institutions. Continuing to use 'Hispanics' as an example, specialized Puerto-Rican shops in New York (*bodegas*) not only carry specialized goods not obtainable elsewhere, they also serve important latent functions as social and information centers. Other examples (some highly counter-intuitive) were discussed earlier. Also among Puerto-Ricans in New York, brightly colored wooden shanties (*casitas*) in community vegetable gardens become gathering places and centers of community life, music, and crafts where children learn traditional dances and music; they become institutions. In this case however, as in others, this may lead to conflicts. *Casitas* are evaluated negatively by other New Yorkers and they also violate building codes, ownership laws, etc.[43] These three points also clearly show the need to define housing in terms of wants and choices, activities and settings, and to consider the larger system of settings (as discussed earlier).

The need for homogeneity and adaptability

The discussion in this chapter means that usually one can expect to find many and often highly diverse groups, although they need to be discovered and identified. This can make design difficult, especially at the neighborhood scale. Open-ended design can help (to be discussed briefly later). It can also be made easier if homogeneous neighborhoods are allowed or encouraged, but, for example, in the U.S. (unlike Canada) it is illegal. Thus, for example, a group of Hmong immigrants in Wisconsin proposed the development of an homogeneous community near Green Bay. This was rejected on constitutional grounds, and there have been major difficulties with attempts to develop Orthodox Jewish communities near New York City. It should be emphasized that historically and cross-culturally, homogeneity can be based on many different criteria: race, religion, caste, occupation, language, kinship, ideology, place of origin, and others (if, as we shall see later, they affect lifestyle). Immigrants in both developed and developing countries often try to cluster using various criteria in order to develop supportive environments. In all these cases, we are dealing with perceived (emic) not imposed (etic) homogeneity. Also, as various populations move and begin to acculturate, many, and often complex, forms of syncretism follow. These lead to new lifestyles, activities, settings, etc. This suggests that design needs to be adaptable. In the postscript, I will briefly discuss the need for open-ended design as one effect on design of considering culture.

Another potentially interesting and useful approach, which has not yet been tried or even investigated, is to apply the idea of constancy and universals (discussed in Chapter 5, see Figures 40 and 41, p. 82 and p. 88, respectively). It might be possible to determine:

Constancy and universals

(i)   What is common,
(ii) What is different but is an expression of what is common, and
(iii) What is *truly* different.

Also, as already mentioned, rates of change could also be investigated and can become immediately useful in design, as is most clearly shown in the case of developing countries.

CHAPTER 7

Making 'Culture' Usable

Given the fact that most of the literature on culture-environment relations deals with and emphasizes the importance of culture and that, as we have seen, there has been a general acceptance in many fields of the importance of culture, one can ask why it has been so little used. As already pointed out, everyone talks about it but no one seems to do anything about it. In this chapter, some possible reasons for this state of affairs are given and some suggestions are made about how one might do something about it — how one might begin to use 'culture' in research, analysis, programming, design, and post-occupancy evaluation.

'Culture' is a concept

The main reason, I suggest, why it has seemed impossible to establish relationships between culture and environment (in this discussion, mainly housing) is due to the very high level of generality and abstraction of the term 'culture.' As already suggested for other concepts like these, e.g., 'environment,' 'activities,' 'vernacular,' 'tradition,' 'environmental quality,' etc., it is essential to dismantle them.[44] This is critical in the case of 'culture,' which is an ideational term, a concept, a definition, which, as we have already seen, has referred, since it was coined in 1871, to all (or most) things that people believe, think, do, or create. As a result, culture is not a 'thing'; no one will ever see culture but only its outcomes and possibly its constituent parts.

The concept of 'culture' is useless

As it stands, therefore, I would suggest the concept of culture is not very useful, either in EBS or design; in fact, it is essentially useless. There are two reasons for this.

The first reason concerns the nature of statements about the relation between culture and environment. These statements tend to assume implicitly that culture and built environments are equivalent units. That is not the case. Culture is a vast domain, built from, however broadly defined it is in any one case, a small part of the whole culture and also a subset of it. The latter is, as it were, embedded in the former. As a result, the nature of the relationships between culture and environment, and the nature of any translation process of one into the other, becomes difficult to grasp. Without resolving either the nature of the relationship or the nature of the translation process at this level, it is essential that this difficulty be born in mind.

The second, and possibly more important (because it can be addressed), reason why 'culture' as such is not useful in either research or design is that it is impossible to use, either to try to understand how environments arise and are used, or to design environments. To be asked to "design for culture" is, I would suggest, an impossible task. To be asked to design an environment for a specific culture (say group A) is still impossible, as is the task of designing a more specific environment (say housing) for group A. The reason is that, as discussed in Chapter 5, 'culture' is a definitional concept, a label as it were, for a vast range of human phenomena. As a result, it is both *too abstract* and *too general* (or global) to be useful. As already suggested, it is often extremely helpful to clarify excessively broad and abstract concepts by *dismantling* them and studying the components and expressions and the ways in which they interrelate with each other and, more importantly, with other variables — in this case, components of built environments.[45] This, in effect, makes the concept operational

and, as I will show later, addresses the nature of the translation process between 'culture' and 'environment'; in fact, it becomes relatively easy.

Over quite a few years I have gradually developed two complementary ways of responding to these twin problems of excessive abstractness and excessive generality.

The first and more recent of these addresses the view that 'culture' is too abstract.

It begins with the frequently found reference to 'socio-cultural' variables, which I used in *House Form and Culture*. It takes the position that

FIGURE 43. Dismantling 'culture' in response to the problem of excessive abstractness (based on Rapoport A (1998) Using "culture" in housing design. *Housing and Society* 25(1/2):8, Fig. 4.).

'social' and 'cultural' are distinct and separable. 'Cultural' is an ideational concept, it is the blueprint for the social variables, which are the more concrete manifestations and outcomes of culture. Important among these are the actual, potentially observable, social expressions of culture, such as family and kinship structure, social networks, roles, statutes, social institutions, and the like. Not only are these potentially observable, they have all been much studied; accepted methods for studying them exist, and there is significant research literature on them in a number of disciplines, such as anthropology, sociology, social psychology, etc. These can, therefore, feasibly be related to built environments, as we will see later, whereas 'culture' cannot.

'Culture' is a theoretical construct

It needs to be reiterated that 'culture' is a theoretical construct. It exists by definition and is a conceptual summary shorthand and a proposed explanation for particular conjunctions of a great variety of human phenomena. As already suggested, no one has ever seen or will ever see or observe culture, only its effects, expressions, or products. One is thus making inferences about an unobservable entity based on observables. This is common (in fact, the norm) in science and presents no insurmountable problems if the nature of this entity is made explicit and is born in mind.

The excessive breadth of 'culture'

To address the second problem, the excessive breadth or global nature of 'culture,' I use another form of dismantling the concept. This I have used, advocated, and gradually developed since the 1970s. This also begins with the observation that it is not possible to link culture and environment at this level of generality. As already discussed, to be asked to analyze the relation between culture and environment, or to 'design for culture,' is to be given an impossible task. As also pointed out earlier, greater specificity, whether with regard to the environment (e.g., housing) or culture (group A), does not help. The proposed dismantling is based on the idea that particular parts or components of the environment (recall that 'environment' is also to be dismantled) are congruent with, or supportive of, particular 'lower-level' components of culture. That depends on having some understanding of the mechanisms involved (which were discussed earlier). While the first dismantling to social variables (see Figure 43, p. 93) is extremely useful, it is also most helpful to derive a sequence of increasingly specific components or expressions of cul-

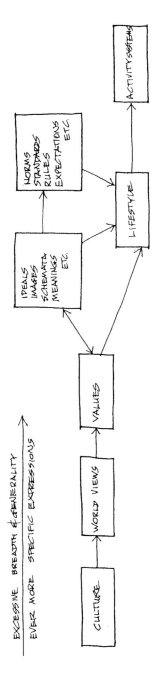

FIGURE 44. Dismantling 'culture' in response to the problem of excessive breadth and generality (based on *op.cit.*, Fig. 5, p. 9).

ture, such as world views, values, images, norms, lifestyles, and activity systems.

Worldviews — the way members of a particular culture (group) 'see' the world — have some utility and there is, in fact, a literature on worldviews. The concept is, however, still rather abstract and not easy to use. One aspect of worldviews is values. These are more specific and more useful. The study of preference and choice discussed earlier is explicitly based on values. One example is studies concerning tradeoffs, which limited resources make necessary in housing choice, and which housing games study. Much of microeconomics is also based on values, and housing and neighborhood choice can be studied in that way; the usefulness of studying advertising is also an aspect of this.

Ideals, images, schemata, etc. Values are often expressed through ideals, images, schemata, meanings, and the like. These in turn lead to certain norms, standards, expectations, rules, etc. These play an important role in the evaluation of environments (see Figure 19, p. 53). They, as well as values, lead to lifestyles.

Lifestyles The concept of lifestyle has proved particularly useful, and I will discuss it in more detail later. It has proved useful for the study of a great variety of environment-behavior interactions, for the design of environments, and for marketing. Lifestyle itself has been defined in many different ways. As in my discussion of culture, these different definitions have been reviewed and an operational definition was proposed in 1970 by Michelson and Reed (in an unpublished report). This proposes that lifestyle be seen as the outcome of choices about how to allocate resources, not only economic but also time, effort, involvement, etc. This I have found most useful, especially since it is related to choice. I have used it, refined it, and developed it and have suggested how it can be represented graphically in the form of profiles and then related to environmental quality profiles (I will discuss that later).

Activity and activity systems Lifestyle in turn leads to activity and activity systems. These are the most concrete expression of culture, and architects and planners are relatively familiar with using activity analysis. However, it is essential that the latent aspects of activities (meaning) be included (see Figure 14, p. 41). Recall that this means that the distinction still made between 'function' and 'meaning' is misconceived, so that meaning is not only an important aspect of function (and activities) but often *the most important function*.[46] This is because specifics of activity systems lead to the specific attributes of settings and environments explaining reasons for their diversity and, as a result, the relation between culture and environment. Together, lifestyle and activity systems are extremely useful in analyzing and designing environments.

These two approaches to dismantling 'culture' (Figures 43 and 44) can usefully be combined into a single diagram (see Figure 45, p. 98).

In it, the width of the arrows suggests the relative feasibility and ease of using the various components and expressions of culture for both analyzing and designing environments. Recall that the links between components of culture and environment are through the various mechanisms discussed earlier. The goal is congruence and supportiveness between users and systems of settings. In fact, the most useful approach is to begin with the variables in the above diagrams, rather than with specific groups because it is relatively easy to link those to environments (as I will show later). It is also the case that these variables themselves help to define groups.

Lifestyle groups are especially useful for several reasons. First, while they are specific enough to be useful, they are more general than activity systems. Second, most other criteria for group membership, such as age, sex, race, ethnicity, caste, tribe, religion, education, occupation, ideology, class, and so on (all of which have been used historically and cross-culturally), can all be expressed in terms of lifestyle.[47] If they cannot, they probably do not affect the appropriateness of environments. Third, as already mentioned, lifestyle is increasingly used in marketing, market segmentation, consumer research, advertising, and housing design by developers. As a result, there is much information available on lifestyle groups that can be purchased from consulting and research organizations, which is not terribly expensive. This provides information about lifestyle groups, the number depending on the particular classification (the 8, 43, or 50 discussed earlier). They describe consumption patterns — food, drink, clothing, transportation, media, books, etc. — recreational and leisure activity systems, as

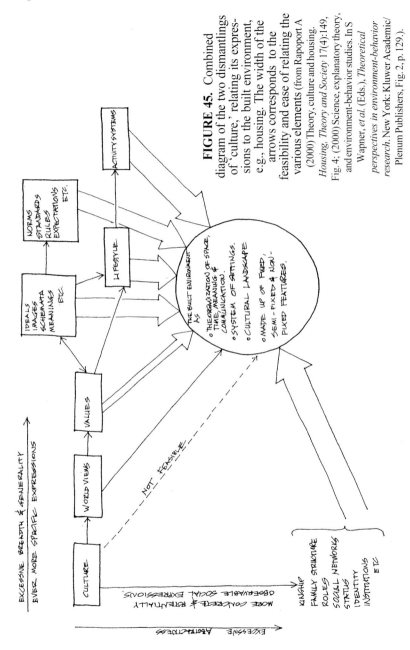

FIGURE 45. Combined diagram of the two dismantlings of 'culture,' relating its expressions to the built environment, e.g., housing. The width of the arrows corresponds to the feasibility and ease of relating the various elements (from Rapoport A (2000) Theory, culture and housing. *Housing, Theory and Society* 17(4):149, Fig. 4; (2000) Science, explanatory theory, and environment-behavior studies. In S Wapner, *et al.* (Eds.), *Theoretical perspectives in environmen-behavior research.* New York: Kluwer Academic/Plenum Publishers. Fig. 2, p. 129.).

well as location, housing, and neighborhood (some are even cross-classified geographically by zip-codes, i.e., postal districts). They also predict attitudes to child rearing, nature, etc., and hence more specific environmental choices (e.g., a better house in a 'worse' neighborhood or the reverse), importance of schools, taxes, etc. In all these ways, lifestyles result in notions of ideal people leading ideal lives in ideal environments. These are often embodied in images, which housing advertisements reflect, and which, within given constraints, guide choice, whether of housing or in design.

There are several other advantages to using lifestyle in analysis and design. Like environmental quality profiles and design, it is a result of choice. Moreover, it shares the term 'style' with design and, as already discussed, style itself, whether of environment or life, is the result of systematic choices among alternatives.[48] Lifestyle can also be represented as a profile. As in the case of environmental quality profiles, four things can vary: the nature of the components, their ranking (relative importance), whether positive (sought) or negative (avoided), and their absolute importance (or magnitude) vis-à-vis other things. This last one is, however, problematic; lifestyle being a more all-embracing concept than environmental quality, it may be difficult to discover components that are not part of it. In any case, it may be possible to match or relate the two profiles — environmental quality and lifestyle. In that way, one might be able to see how the lifestyle of a group is reflected in the environmental quality of the system of settings. One can easily image and show the two profiles overlapping, or better, facing each other (one being 'reversed'). Whether that is also possible with polar profiles is not clear. (See Figure 46, p. 100.)

Lifestyle represented as a profile

Potentially, this is most useful in planning and design, in programming and evaluation, and in research. One could see whether or not particular lifestyle profiles are reflected in environmental quality profiles. One might be able to begin to detect patterns, which are a first step in research, generalization, and theory building and can help with prediction. As in the case of environmental quality, one can also study the effect of various constraints on feasibility.

As in the case for 'activities' and 'lifestyle,' most (or many) of the expressions of culture often need further disman-

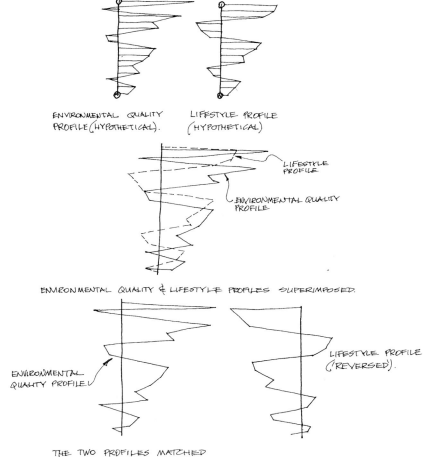

FIGURE 46. Environmental quality and lifestyle profile (redrawn from Rapoport A (1995) Environmental quality and environmental quality profiles. In A Rapoport (Ed.), *Thirty-three papers in environment-behavior research*. Newcastle, U.K.: Urban International Press, Fig. 6, p. 482 and Fig. 7, p. 485.).

tling, as does 'environment.' Recall that dismantling is a *general* strategy. Thus, for example, values, ideals, images, schemata, etc., and norms, standards, rules etc., all need to be made more specific, usually by dismantling.[49] Similarly, the social expressions of culture are clearly still too broad and need to be dismantled; it is the specifics of kinship, family structure, roles, social networks, status, identity, and institutions that are important and can be relatively easily linked to environments.

CHAPTER 8

Examples of Application

I now provide some examples to support my claim that whereas it is impossible to relate 'culture' to any built environment (e.g., housing as defined earlier in this book), it is easy to do so using the expression of culture shown in Figures 43, 44, and 45 on pp. 93, 95, and 98, respectively, especially those with wide arrows, and I will use some examples already discussed. The examples used are not meant to be exhaustive. They cannot be because much of the EBS research literature can be used. The number of examples becomes much larger still when, in addition, the popular media can be used to provide an almost endless supply from advertising, newspaper stories, novels, TV, film, popular music, and so on.[50] One can also use the fairly inexpensive databases on the various lifestyle groups mentioned earlier.[51] This makes it much easier to broaden the body of evidence, to develop lateral connections and conceptual frameworks, and to integrate and synthesize diverse material on the way to theory development.

Variables do interact

In beginning to show how the variables derived by dismantling 'culture' can be used, it needs to be emphasized that although these variables can be separated and, in principle, ranked in terms of their importance, they do interact. Although that complicates matters, it also makes it easier to relate them, helping with synthesis. Note that not only can group differences be identified and used but there is also possible convergence due to changing values, standards, images, and the like, as in the case of the suburban image discussed earlier. It is significant that this trend can so far be found in the media rather than the research literature.

Discussion of Figures 43 and 44

I first discuss the *horizontal axis* (Figure 44, p. 95), which addresses the problems of excessive breadth and generality. The more specific expressions I discuss are values — ideals, images, schemata and meanings, norms, standards, expectations, rules, etc. — lifestyle, and activity systems. Along *the vertical axis* (Figure 43, p. 93), the more concrete expressions of culture that I discuss are kinship, family structure, roles, social networks, status, identity, and institutions. Because after dismantling 'environment' I use four fairly general conceptualizations of it, it is possible to apply the process I use for housing to other types of environment.

Along the *horizontal axis* I begin with *values*. These describe how people value various 'goods' so that they play an important role in microeconomics. As a result, they have been much studied in advertising and marketing, including housing. Because values lead to differences in resource allocation, they are immediately and directly linked to lifestyle. Since most people's resources are limited, tradeoffs must always be made; housing and community games enable this to be studied. Tradeoffs are, of course, central in the choices made in design (see Figures 28, 32, and 33, pp. 66, 68, and 70, respectively) and, as a result, so are values (for example, designers' as opposed to users'). In the case of housing, values lead to the differential importance of the dwelling (as a building) versus the neighborhood, location within the settlement, taxes, microclimate, school quality, social characteristics of neighbors, and so on, helping explain the choices made by various groups. Values, of course, also help to define groups and are transmitted during the enculturation of children (ensuring cultural continuity and survival of groups). This process depends partly on dwellings and how they are used. This links any discussion of values to family, kinship, and even social networks, since in some cultures non-kin play an important role in enculturation.

The horizontal axis — values

This discussion could be continued at length;[52] it shows how easily lateral connections among variables can be made, and I encourage readers to make connections to material in earlier parts of the book, e.g., The Australian Green Streets Project. I will, however, conclude with an example which relates this discussion to a study of housing subdivisions (developments) in the U.S. and, in this way also, with the convergence on the suburban image in other countries. In this study of 5,000 prospective house buyers in California, Florida, Georgia, North Carolina, and Texas, various amenities were ranked based on the percentage of people who wanted them. Not only could this be expressed as an environmental quality profile but it provides a clear guide to planners and designers when making tradeoffs.

TABLE 1. Ranking of amenities desired in a sample of 5,000 prospective house buyers in the U.S. from the Urban Land Institute.

Natural open space	77%
Walking and biking paths	74%
Gardens	56%
Convenience stores	55%
Wilderness areas	52%
Outdoor swimming pool	52%
Community/recreation center	52%
Shopping center	51%
Interesting little parks	50%
Town center with shops, coffee bars, and meeting places	48%
Neighborhood recreation activities	47%
Library	47%
Places of worship	46%
Tennis courts	39%
Golf course	39%
Teen center	36%
Golf clubhouse	33%
Amphitheater	26%
Organizer to start clubs and community events	23%
Community concierge	18%

Cited in Wiechman L (1997) More than a neighborhood: New homeowners demanding big-ticket items from developers. *Milwaukee Journal Sentinel* 30 Nov.

Advertisements are useful for studying culture

Values are often expressed through ideals, images, schemata, meanings, and the like. This is why advertisements and popular media are so useful and important, as I have already suggested.[53] Not only are they extremely numerous and found all over the world (making cross-cultural studies possible) but it is also possible, by looking at advertising aimed at different groups, to easily study differences within countries (as a number of student papers have shown). Such advertisements also respond quickly, almost instantaneously, to changes in the various expressions of culture, so that 'culture change' can be followed as it occurs. I will discuss two examples very briefly.

The first concerns the revival of downtown living in the U.S. In Milwaukee, Wisconsin, where I live, an area that has been particularly attractive is called the *Historic* Third Ward (the name is itself suggestive). In what had been a warehouse and industrial area, advertisements emphasize "a prestigious lifestyle," linking images to lifestyle and status: "Milwaukee at your doorstep," "art galleries," "theaters," "Lake Michigan," "fantastic views," "shopping" and "chic shops," "entertainment," "stylish restaurants," and so on. An image is built up that describes a particular lifestyle and environmental quality attractive to a particular group.

My second example of the power of images is the suburban house and its surroundings, already discussed. Examples are found in Bangkok (Thailand), Japan, Russia, Turkey, African countries, Latin America, and so on. In Indonesia, an article in the *Los Angeles Times* described new developments in Jakarta as looking like Southern California. A sales pamphlet from a new development in Jogjakarta is striking. The development is called *Merapi View* and described as "*exclusive and nostalgic*"; the use of an English name is very significant and often found. A suburban image is projected and except for Indonesian text in parts, the houses are difficult to distinguish from those elsewhere, even when described as "Indisch" (Indian!) — a Dutch term! — or "vernacular." The facilities advertised (in English!) include a tennis court, fitness center, clubhouse, restaurant, mini-market, drug store, jogging track, playground, swimming pool, 24-hour security, satellite TV dishes, underground wiring, telephone, and air-conditioning. This is similar to the environmental quality profile described in the United States (see Table 1 on the previous page), as are the ideals, images, etc. In this case, however, they help explain not cultural differences but convergence, possibly based on the input of images in the mass media, the high status of "modernity," and so on.

Expectations, norms, standards, and rules

Values, images, and the like lead to certain 'expectations,' and thus norms, standards, and rules, not only those expressed through design but also those that link settings and behavior. In design the application of rules to achieve certain norms and standards leads to choices being made that result in environments that approach the ideals as closely as possible, given various constraints. These norms, standards, and rules are also used in the evaluation of environments.

One example has already been discussed — the different evaluations of the *casitas* used by Puerto Ricans in New York. The role of norms, standards, and behavioral rules in evaluation may lead to areas being defined as 'slums' with inappropriate actions resulting, e.g., redevelopment. One particular neighborhood in Los Angeles was defined as a slum because a particular group of people (Russian immigrants), their dress, use of streets and other spaces, levels of house maintenance, and other cues did not correspond to those acceptable to Anglo-Americans. It is well known that, generally, norms regarding materials, colors, house-styles, plants used, and standards of house maintenance, lawn care, etc. often lead to major conflicts. In relatively homogeneous (by lifestyle) areas, they lead to specific ambience (see Figure 42, p. 89). It is this ambience that is then evaluated.

Norms and standards regarding lighting levels, comfort (e.g., temperature), amount of space, privacy, spacing (and hence density), and many other variables have a major impact on design and the acceptability of resulting environments. One example already mentioned is that in the U.S., at the same time that family size is decreasing, the size of houses is increasing, and the average new house is now over 3000 square feet (300 sq. m.). The determinant is clearly space standards and norms and rules about privacy, reflecting values, ideals, images, etc.

The systematic application of rules, as we have seen, by guiding the choice among alternatives, leads to styles and the identity of cultural landscapes, their ambience. As we have also seen, rules can be written or unwritten, formal or informal, and conflicts may occur between group-specific informal rules and formal rules, such as codes and regulations. By applying rules, the various expressions of culture are translated into built environments; specific rules also help define groups by guiding behavior in settings, defining what is appropriate or acceptable, where, when, and among which people. In one study of a U.S. suburb, as just one example, unwritten rules make most behaviors generally inappropriate in public settings and there is no public space (see footnote 31). The difference between such a suburb, or the U.S. generally, and say a street in India is overwhelming.[54] As one says colloquially, they represent two very different cultures. In my terms, they reflect two different lifestyles in terms of appropriate behavior in public spaces; they also reflect two very different schemata of what is public (and, therefore, private) space and the gradations among them (semi-public, semi-private, etc.)

Clearly the rules above refer to norms and standards of behavior, about what one does and does not do, where, when, and with whom; these also reflect an 'ideal.' Thus, since lifestyle is also the result of choice, such rules link norms and standards to lifestyle. Although I have suggested that, in EBS, lifestyle is possibly the most helpful expression of culture, it is rather different to some of the others; it is made up of many specific components and can be expressed as a profile (like environmental quality). This means not only that it requires more dismantling than the other variables, but that only a few examples can be given *within* that expression of culture.

Consider a simple example that depends on how people use their free time. If one spends the same amount of free time in restaurants, watching TV, foreign travel, jogging, following a hobby (internet, gardening, hunting and fishing, etc.), reading, etc., the choices regarding location in the city, neighborhood, essential settings outside the dwelling, and nature of the dwelling will all be different, as will their relative importance. If one works at home, requirements are different still. The lifestyle of singles, young married couples, parents with children, single parents, and people with grown up children would all be different, with very different needs and wants. As these categories cross-cut many others, the number of lifestyle groups goes up, as discussed earlier. It is precisely these that the commercial databases describe, and that have been used extensively by housing developers in the U.S. The examples that follow are from developers' 'trade literature.'

Many of these groups have catchy (and often humorous) names attached to them, a kind of shorthand sometimes even illustrated by stereotypical characters. Some examples are "Yuffies" (young urban failures) as distinguished from the better-known "yuppies" (young urban professionals). These labels vary among the different databases. One with 48 lifestyles refers to "suburban gentry," "nouveau riche," "tuition and braces" (i.e., with teenage children), "urban gentry," and so on. Another classification, illustrated with drawings of house exteriors and interiors, and describing both the facilities and images wanted, are "unyuppies," whose values differ from yuppies but who appear similar. There are "yappies" (young aspiring professionals), "treaders," "YMCAs" (young married childless achievers), "scampies" (societally conscious affluent mature parents),

Linking norms and standards to lifestyle

Group names and their lifestyles

107

and so on. The housing, neighborhood, and locational preferences of each group are described.

For each of the groups, income, leisure activities, the products and amenities they buy, their pets (if any), what they eat, drink, read, and other specifics of their lifestyles are provided. In discussing these, the housing developers' trade literature and the proprietary databases provide suggestions for marketing approaches. Other such classifications, each with detailed profiles, use 8, 37, 43, or 47 lifestyle groups, sometimes grouped into more general categories (nine in the case of the 43 above). In addition, geographical location at the regional scale and by postal districts is often provided to aid marketing. Clearly the proliferation of such data and their use in housing development, design, and marketing is convincing evidence for its utility and importance. It would be very useful if architects and urban and landscape designers analyzed this material in order to see how useful it might be and, also, in order to be able to work with developers and possibly improve design.

Lifestyles result in activity systems   As Figures 44 and 45 on pp. 95 and 98 show, lifestyles result in activity systems. These are the most concrete and specific and link lifestyles (and ultimately culture) with built environments. Since I have already used cooking and kitchens (e.g., among Puerto Ricans and Apache) as an example of the impact of latent aspects, it is useful to use some recent examples to show how lifestyle affects kitchen design in terms of instrumental aspects. The same examples also show the role of constraints in making it difficult or impossible to satisfy some of the special requirements identified, due either to conflicts with codes and regulations, economics, or politics.

Examples of how lifestyle affects design   The example is from Britain where there is now provision for "ethnic housing," which, however, ignores subgroups. Two groups, Chinese and Bangladeshis, are discussed. Chinese people prefer cooking with gas for greater control. Gas, however, is not allowed in multi-story buildings in Britain (note that the use of high-rise housing is probably itself a result of economic constraints). Food storage is important in Chinese kitchens (as it is in the case of other minority ethnic groups); larger kitchens are needed, which raises costs. Cooking methods produce much steam and oil smoke so that heavy-duty extractive fans are needed, which cost more. In addition elsewhere, there is a need for specific color and window shapes for symbolic reasons and specific spatial needs due to higher levels of socializing than among the British. In the case of Bangladeshis, the use of cooking fat and spices and the need to feed large households and many guests leads to much condensation, which needs special extraction fans. Ideally, catering size cookers and sinks are also needed. Kitchens need to be large, also because of the need for storage of bulk products. Large households obviously have other spatial implications. Due to religious requirements, separate living and eating areas are needed for men and women. Privacy preventing women from visiting male guests requires specific forms of space organization. The need for ritual ablutions leads to specific bathroom requirements, which cost more.

Lifestyle differences among Muslim, Chinese, and Hindu populations in Singapore would ideally have an impact on many aspects of apartment design also. The provision of standardized apartments means that *people* have to adapt to dwellings, rather than dwellings to people. Because of politics, it is believed that housing for the three groups must be identical. Canada, on the other hand, does encourage culture-specific housing. Very specific housing needs follow from the lifestyles and activities of Chinese and Vietnamese residents.[55] Other examples discussed earlier are also relevant to the present discussion. I encourage readers to try and relate them and also to develop their own examples.

One final point. In the case of the Puerto Ricans in New York discussed earlier (see footnote 9) and the cases discussed above, kitchens are just one of the settings that are affected by activity systems, including their latent aspects. This also applies to living rooms, bedrooms, entrances, relationships among settings, relation of settings to the outdoors, and thus window placement, and so on. As already seen, the relationships among dwellings are also affected, as in the case of Hispanics in Arizona or the case of Feng Shui in areas with large Chinese populations (California in the U.S. and Manchester in Britain).

I now turn to the *vertical axis* (Figures 43 and 45, pp. 93 and 98), which addresses the problem of excessive abstractness. Along this axis, and considering the more concrete expressions of culture, I begin with kinship. I then discuss family structure, roles, social networks, status, identity, and

The vertical axis — excessive abstractness

social institutions. Note two things: first, this list is not complete; second, the order is not hierarchical, these variables are *not* in order of importance.

Kinship and housing

Concerning *kinship*, I have already given some examples: Hispanics in the U.S. and the English working class in London in the 1950s. The examples above of the Chinese and Bangladeshis in Britain and of Hispanics in the U.S. are at least partly related to the importance of kinship. We have also seen that much higher densities can be tolerated by Chinese if kin are involved then when strangers are involved, and that the definition of 'kin' among both Chinese and Mexicans is much broader than among Anglo-Americans.

In general, kinship seems to play a larger role in the housing of traditional societies than it does currently, especially in developed countries. As a result, identifying kinship patterns is indispensable to understanding housing there and to design supportive housing. The major impact in such situations is through clustering so that kinship becomes an important form of homogeneity at the neighborhood level. In such cases, kinship also helps explain settlement form, street pattern and use, and housing clusters (or compounds). It also has an impact on house forms, such as communal dwellings, or the ability to use densely clustered courtyard housing (as in the Middle East), sometimes without even the commonly used narrow streets (which become semi-private space). Access is instead directly among houses. Traditional kinship clusters can persist, albeit in new forms, such as the 'family circle' in Scandinavia. The reduced importance of kinship in housing may also be reversed, either 'naturally' or through design. The aging of many populations may lead to the use of 'grannie flats' and their equivalents, as in Australia and Japan. It also leads to new forms of housing, such as various forms of co-housing. Other responses include houses shared by unrelated young and old, or by single-parent families. Such arrangements can be seen as a form of 'fictitious kinship' found in some traditional societies. It can also be seen as a link between kinship and *family structure*, the boundary between which can be difficult to determine. At the same time, multigenerational households can cause conflicts and problems, especially for men and teenagers. These conflicts seem to be due to values, ideals, expectations, lifestyles, and activity systems.

Family structure has been seen for quite some time as a useful way of relating culture to housing. Clearly the dwelling as the primary setting and focus of family life needs to be congruent with the numbers and organization of the household. Although family structure would clearly not be relevant in the case of certain settings — offices, industry, research, etc. — it will play a role in others. These would include settings that form part of the relevant system of settings that is housing, but may include settings that *a priori* seem unlikely to be related. One example is health facilities where, in certain cases, the patient's whole family may be present and involved. Another may be airports. These, when many family members accompany or await passengers, may have specific spatial requirements.

In the case of housing, as in all cases of EBR, the interaction of family and housing is two-way: family type and organization influence dwellings and the latter in turn have effects in the family. This is particularly the case when there are time lags — changes in the family are not reflected in the housing, which becomes inhibiting. As will be discussed in the post-script, that is one of the reasons for the need for open-ended design.

It is also the case that, in general, the household and family are one and the same. There are clearly exceptions, although even in extreme cases, such as communal dwellings (which are also settlements), the family (however defined) still forms the basic unit, the building block, as it were, of the dwelling community. It is, therefore, most important to consider the family when dealing with housing, particularly since many current changes in housing (and even settlement) form and use are intimately related to various changes in the nature of the family unit, which also affects lifestyle, roles, activity systems, etc. This is the case with changes (or differences) in family structure, for example, single parent, working couples, extended families, co-housing groups, young and elderly, single person households, large families, polygamous families, etc. These have implications not only for the dwelling, for example, its size, kitchens, living rooms, etc., but because housing is a system of settings, there are also implications for urban form. For example, smaller households increase the area of housing because kitchens, bathrooms, parking, etc. still need to be provided; density is thus reduced. On the other hand, large families often lead to higher densities

Family structure and housing

through the opposite process and the need for large houses. Thus, in the case of an Hasidic Jewish community in Brooklyn, family, and hence housing size, has led to special zoning, allowing coverage of 65% of the lot with reduced setbacks and backyards. There are also many changes and additions, which lead to the need for open-endedness as the family changes over time. Although this is not related to family *per se*, the specifics of the religion have major impacts on the design of the dwelling, especially kitchens, the nature of many highly specific settings, and how they are arranged in the neighborhood, including their extent, i.e., on the Sabbath one must walk.

In the U.S. state of Utah, there are still polygamous families among Mormons. This requires, in one case, 10 bedrooms, 7 bathrooms, 2 kitchens, 2 nurseries, 2 laundry rooms, and a school room. There are, of course, still polygamous families in the Middle East, Africa, and elsewhere. In those cases due to family *size,* space becomes the major concern, as it does for the Hasidim discussed above. This applies both to initial size and to how easily dwellings can be expanded. The differences in the *structure* of families in the different cases led to very different housing forms and use.

Family is also important because it is a most important 'intermediate institution' that helps people cope with difficult (and stressful) situations. It thus becomes particularly important in situations of 'high criticality,' e.g., urban migrants, immigrants, rapid culture change, etc. Also recall that the dwelling and family are central in enculturation and, therefore, play a central role in the cultural continuity and survival of groups. There are also groups in which all adult members have the authority to control children's behavior in public spaces and settings. When design makes this impossible, delinquency and other problems often arise. All these and other aspects of housing/family relationships have been studied. Clearly, linking family to design is relatively easy, whereas linking 'culture' is impossible.

Changed roles affect the organization and use of settings

Change in family structure has an impact on *roles*, but so do other forces. The different definition of roles among different groups (i.e., 'cultures') has major (although not the only) effects on the organization and use of settings at many scales. Roles probably have both a constant and variable component so that when considered over time and cross-culturally, both patterns and differences and variations will be found. At the settlement scale, changing women's roles (e.g., employment) has resulted in a 50% increase in women's driving and has been largely responsible for the growth of traffic in London. However, male driving did not increase. This was partly due to work but also to the perceived benefits of cars (and hence reduced use of public transport).[56] For example, it is easier to take children to and from school and to shop when one also works. In this case, then, changed roles have led to changes in lifestyle, activity systems, etc. and in the organization of time and space.

In Moslem societies, the very different roles of males and females lead to very different home ranges and use of various settings, with major impacts on dwellings, shopping, neighborhood, and other settings — educational, medical, etc. As roles change with 'modernization' and 'westernization' or the opposite (as in Iran and Afghanistan), so do the setting systems required. These have been studied in various countries and, for example, in Portugal it has been found that changes in sex roles influence house types and space use both inside and outside the dwelling.

There is a rapidly growing body of research on the impact of home-based employment, especially among women, on the design and use of dwellings, the impact on neighborhood, and the development and use of other settings within the neighborhood. We have already seen that the response to one such setting, child care, differs among different groups as in the case of Hispanics discussed earlier.

As a last example, consider the changed roles that follow the increase in two-job families. One question is: Who takes care of the dwelling when both spouses have careers? Various responses can be found: men may take on new tasks or, as is often the case, women maintain traditional household roles while working, although substantial changes were beginning to occur by the mid 1980s in the U.S., with clear links to family/housing relationships. Another set of responses has been a lowering of standards of cleanliness and housekeeping or using outside cleaners. The details of all the changes are less important here than the fact that these various processes occur and have a direct impact on housing, including other settings in the system such as the use of restaurants, prepared foods (shops), child care facilities, and so on. Even more important is the fact that not only is it relatively easy to trace such relationships between roles and changes in roles and housing, but that there are also indirect effects via values, family structure, and all the other aspects (or expressions) of culture.

Social networks — intensive or extensive? In discussing kinship and family structure, one type of *social network* has already been mentioned. More generally, there is an extensive, cross-cultural, well-established literature on social networks. This research began in the 1960s among British anthropologists working in Africa. Social networks can be with neighbors, friends, and kin on the basis of common interests, ideology, lifestyle, language, caste, place of origin, occupation, religion, tribe, ethnicity, and other forms of perceived homogeneity. Not only is the literature extensive but there are well-developed methods to study social networks, classifications of network types, etc. This provides a valuable and easy way to relate 'culture' to the systems of settings linked to the dwelling. I have already discussed some examples, such as shops, markets, clubs, coffee and tea houses, bars, etc., when dealing with latent aspects of a variety of settings as places of social interaction. An important aspect not yet discussed and also neglected in research on social networks is their spatial extent, whether they are intensive — local, based mainly on proximity, and thus largely restricted to the neighborhood — or extensive — based on shared interests, lifestyles, activities, hobbies, work, etc., and thus spatially widespread.

It has been frequently argued that the former are being replaced by the latter. Although in general that seems to be happening, there are major differences among groups with the persistence of local networks and even a reversal to them.[57] There are two major classes of reasons for this general change. One is social change, briefly discussed below, the other is technological change.

Technology has clearly had the effect of increasing the spatial extent of networks. As transportation modes have changed, networks have become much more extensive; cars have obviously had the greatest effect, but air-travel has also played a role. Telephones also have helped to enable networks to be maintained over much larger distances, even among family and kin. An interesting, and currently much discussed (and researched), question concerns the possible effects of computers and computer networks.

As is often the case, developing countries clearly show the impact of social change (and also suggest the need to modulate or moderate such change). A good example is Kirtipur, Nepal, recently studied in some detail that shows the joint effects of social and land use change.[58] In the past, neighborhoods were homogeneous, based on caste (as is the case in India and elsewhere in South Asia). Caste was more important in Hindu (as opposed to Buddhist) areas and led to a finer grain of organization and clustering. At the larger scale, religion, as well as caste, was important, and both Buddhist and Hindu populations clustered around their respective religious institutions. Traditionally, these two together rigidly fixed social position and ritual status, which in turn were important in religious rituals, social organization, marriage, personal relations, etc., and hence social networks. These latter were neighborhood centered and based on strong ties. Currently they are weakening and even disappearing in favor of (nuclear) family-centered, dwelling-oriented, private relations, which are due not only to social changes but also to new dwelling forms; again, there is a two-way relationship, as was also found in Turkey and elsewhere. Such private, dwelling-oriented relations reach the ultimate among one of the groups in the case of the suburb discussed earlier (see footnote 31).

The nature of social networks may also change with circumstances. For example, among immigrants, religion or caste may be replaced by place of origin, enabling a small group to establish solidarity, identity, and mutual support. Social networks also vary with lifestyle, so that in a single community, two groups may vary greatly. For one group, it is the absence of networks that is typical not only among houses at the neighborhood (meso) level but even within dwellings. For the other groups, networks are still very important. The first group can also be contrasted with others for whom social networks are primary, such as Australian aborigines, Navajo, Mexicans, etc. An important role of social networks is supportiveness. It follows that as criticality goes up, whether due to migrant status, age, health, resources, prejudice, etc., such networks become more important. In other words, one can not only explain various residential patterns but also begin to predict their occurrence and importance with implications for policy and design.

Group-specific institutions Note that social networks, whether intensive or extensive, are usually centered on the dwelling. They may, however, also be anchored by various group-specific institutions. This relates social networks not only to systems of settings but also to certain *institutions* to which identity and supportiveness may be related.

Religious institutions have already been mentioned, as in the case of Kirtipur above. These are frequently important and differ greatly among groups. For example, in the case of the Orthodox Jewish (Hassidic) community discussed earlier, religious schools, synagogues, kosher shops, and ritual baths are essential. These are highly group-specific and often the reason for clustering (as is also the case for other groups and *their* institutions). In this case, the clustering needs to be tight and the networks intensive because religious rules against driving on the Sabbath influence lifestyle and the extent of systems of activities. In other cases, religious institutions may lead to extensive networks, as is the case of the respective churches for Samoans and Serbs in Los Angeles. Their members live throughout the city but have the (car-related) mobility to use these institutions as their center. It is important to reiterate that specific institutions may be related to identity, and as the latter is created (or recreated), specific institutions take on that role. Among African Americans (as for the Samoans and Serbs) it is churches, whereas for American Indian groups it is cultural centers.

Elsewhere I have discussed the role of tea-shops in Korea, coffee houses in Turkey, and earlier I discussed the role of *bodegas* and *casitas* among Puerto Ricans in New York. I have also commented on the often counter-intuitive nature of the role of certain settings based on latent functions, such as outdoor markets in Mexico, stables in Hungarian villages, and others. These then have to be identified because they become important institutions and consequently become important in the system of settings, which would be considered *a priori*. One example is the importance of group-specific drinking establishments for men (pubs in Britain, taverns in the U.S. and Austria), which are described as their 'living rooms.' Coffee houses in Moslem societies and wine shops in Austrian villages are among other equivalent institutions. I have already discussed the particularly striking example of the town dump on Nantucket Island, Massachusetts, which for 60 years has served as the community center, trading post, or party hall. Its importance as an institution and centrality as a setting only became apparent when it was to be closed, and had serious social implications.

Another example of the latent social role of institutions are book shops and museums in New York City. These have become important settings for meeting single people with similar, and hence compatible, values, lifestyles, and interests. In 1985 *The New York Times* described the courtship rituals that occur in these settings, which attract intellectual, like-minded people who would not use singles bars, which attract very different groups (or laundromats in Australia that have played a similar role). It is worth noting that the groups are identified by the particular settings that they occupy and use. It should also be clear that the role of various settings as important institutions needs to be *discovered,* rather than assumed.

Housing is important in communicating *status* but so are other built environments, such as shops, hotels, office buildings, and others. Neighborhoods and areas of cities also communicate status, as do many other items of material culture (clothing, cars, watches, and others discussed below). This is particularly the case in contemporary societies, such as the U.S., Australia, and the like, without rigid status categories. Its increasing importance in communicating status can be observed in India. There, traditional Brahmin groups with fixed status do not use dwellings to communicate their high status, whereas the new elites do. The two groups communicate status differently and hence use resources differently, i.e., have different lifestyles. This can cause conflict, as was discovered in Colombia where one poor group used resources to improve their residential environment and another did not. In this case involving urban migrants, this also had an impact on adaptation and acculturation.

Communicating status through housing

In cases where housing is used to communicate status, it is striking how apparently clear and self-evident such communication is. For example, in a novel there is a description of a settlement in California ("Pacific Point"), which uses the location and types of houses and other built envi-

117

ronments to communicate status to the extent that it is said to be "divided neatly into social tiers, like something a sociologist had built to prove a theory."[59] An equally unselfconscious, self-evident reading of status (which is why I argued earlier that popular media is so useful), in this case using respectability as the criterion, is in an English novel.[60] Two policemen, in discussing an area, list a series of cues that communicate respectability and status, and the author comments that a conference of town-planners would have taken much longer to identify these components of "suburban delight." Among these are "a nice, quiet neighborhood, decent houses, trees on the footpath, no through traffic and just local vehicles, grass verges, good gardens, near the tennis club," and so on. Note two things: (1) "nice," "decent," "good" are concepts that consist of possibly large sets of cues and, therefore, need dismantling; (2) that this is also, in effect, an environmental quality profile. It has also been found that despite 'culture change,' built environments continue to communicate status (and thus some forms of identity) for surprisingly long periods. In one study in Boston, 19th century houses continued to effectively communicate high status in the late 1980s.

Material culture communicates status

I have mentioned that material culture can generally communicate status. That may be communicated through modern forms and materials (such as concrete, metal window-frames, etc.), which will be discussed below, but very importantly, also by semi-fixed elements, such as cars, motorcycles, TVs, satellite dishes, cordless telephones, etc., and also furniture, furnishings, and decorations. I have argued for some time the importance of materials in communicating status. Recently, this has been studied empirically for the first time: materials clearly have meaning, both intrinsic and culturally specific, so that constancy and variability both play a role. The social meaning of materials (among other things) can also help define social identity (to be discussed below). In many developing countries traditional materials (bamboo, mud brick, and thatch) are rejected due to their meaning as traditional and hence poor and substandard materials. In some developed countries there may be status differences between timber and stone (as in Scotland) or brick, leading to the common use of brick veneer over timber houses (as in Australia, the U.S., etc.). Many multi-story buildings, such as apartments, are timber structures but seem to be built of concrete and brick.

One also finds, as I have during much travel, that in villages in developing countries, manufactured paint with new colors, as well as new materials and forms, are used first by high-status individuals. Color can also be used for identity, as in identifying Moslem houses in parts of India (e.g., at Jamshedpur) or as in the case of conflicts between Portuguese immigrants (who use very bright colors) and locals in Toronto and Montreal; I have already discussed the case of Mexicans in the U.S. The use of the full spectrum of cues — new materials, new styles and forms, height, glazed windows, color, plants and landscaping, furniture, decorations, appliances, etc. — tends to be used by high-status individuals and groups and then 'trickles down' over time, sometimes over long periods of time, as was the case in India where it is still not complete. A comparable example is the use of a western (Paladian) style by elites in 19th century Cairo, Egypt, although in this case the traditional Cairene organization and use of space are found. In effect, the new forms connote social prestige and status, but traditional ideas about family privacy, female modesty, family structure, and guest reception persist. This shows syncretism, which is still to be found (and to be encouraged) in developing countries.

A good example of the joint action of multiple cues to communicate status and miscommunication due to using one's own cues in judging another group is a description of the area of Beijing in which Chinese communist leaders live. This description in *The New York Times* in 1997 shows how, by being matched against the expectations, values, ideals, images, norms, etc. of the correspondent, surprise is expressed 'naturally' that important, high-status people would live in an area which is "a maze of dusty lanes and grubby back alleys … [with blank walls] … punctuated by simple red doorways befitting ramshackle homes." It is then emphasized that behind these doors lie "elegant and spacious courtyard dwellings" and reference is made to the contrast between the limousines (visiting Deng Xiao Ping's family after his death) and the "dirt-and-cobblestone lane." This is clearly a result of the expectation that dwellings should communicate status and also the role of new standards, materials, etc. (see Figure 19, p. 53). It is also a description of a negative environmental quality profile.

Multiple cues and miscommunication of status

This latter topic is also picked up in the description of a new town in China, Zhangjagang, seen as the "nation's ideal" (also in *The New York Times* in 1997). The photograph looks like a Scandinavian housing area with two-story, outward-looking buildings with pitched roofs. The emphasis is on "clean living"— clean streets and lawns and shrubbery (rare in China). The town is said to reflect a "new set of values," which communicates prosperity, shows obedience to the law, is clean and orderly, and fully modern. Sidewalks are of spotted red tile, there is a pedestrian shopping street, parking is controlled, and there are strict rules about garbage. In fact, new residents are given a handbook about how to act, and they describe the town as "a nice place to live." This positive environmental quality profile is implicitly being contrasted with the negative profile of the traditional Beijing neighborhood.

Hassan Fathy's well-known example of New Gurnia failed, I think, at least partly because of the use of mud-brick and a form derived from Nubia, a low status area of Egypt. It is significant that his private houses for wealthy clients with the same characteristics have proved highly successful. The significance of the use of mud-brick is well-illustrated by another unselfconscious use of the correspondent's values, standards, images, etc. in a story about an Egyptian village (in *The New York Times* in 1994). The photo caption refers to a village "so poor that houses are built with mud brick." In the text, point is made that "unable even to afford cement, the 50,000 villages in Gharb al Banawaan area still live in mud-and-wattle homes with dirt-floors."

Identity and culture

In discussing status I have already referred to *identity* several times; they are related, because high-status is one particular type of identity. The many different groups discussed earlier, as well as individual members, all need to establish identity and also maintain it (through enculturation of offspring). This is one of the key roles of culture. The point has already been made that, currently, identity is a much more complex matter than in the past, sometimes with overlapping membership in a number of groups, with more choice and a greater emphasis on individual identity. This leads to more variation within groups than in traditional situations (see Figure 47, p. 121).

This makes the personalization of housing and, therefore, open-ended design (discussed in the postscript) more im-

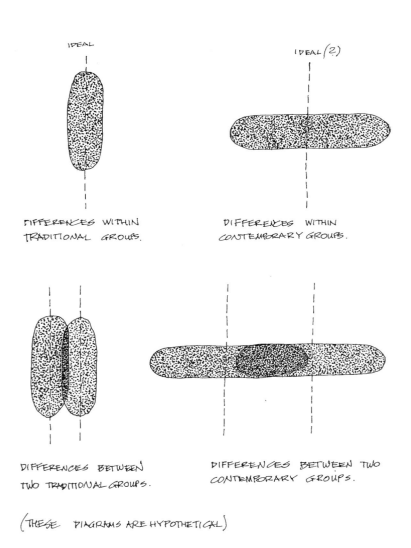

IDEAL

IDEAL (2)

DIFFERENCES WITHIN TRADITIONAL GROUPS.

DIFFERENCES WITHIN CONTEMPORARY GROUPS.

DIFFERENCES BETWEEN TWO TRADITIONAL GROUPS.

DIFFERENCES BETWEEN TWO CONTEMPORARY GROUPS.

(THESE DIAGRAMS ARE HYPOTHETICAL)

FIGURE 47. Differences within and among groups
(from Rapoport A (1990) Systems of activities and systems of settings.
In S Kent (Ed.), *Domestic architecture and the use of space.*
Cambridge: Cambridge University Press, Fig. 2.2, p. 12.).

portant. As suggested in Figure 42 on p. 89, in the case of an homogeneous area, the individual personalizations have enough in common to 'add up' and to produce a specific cultural landscape and ambience (including non-visual components, such as sounds and smells), which together communicate identity. We have already seen that *casitas* and *bodegas* in New York City became identified with Puerto Ricans. I have also already discussed the use of a specific arrangement of furnishings and decorations (an 'aesthetic complex') that were used for identity inside public housing in Boston. Since exteriors could not be modified, cars and clothing were used. In Germany also, where Turks live in apartments, car decorations and specific flowers in flower boxes were used for identity. Plant materials and their organization in front gardens are widely used in many areas to communicate identity. So are fences and other elements. In the Southwestern United States, a particular 'housescape' identifies Mexican Americans. Elements of this cultural landscape include front property enclosure using fences (as opposed to their absence), plant materials, the use of occasional religious shrines, and the use of brilliant and specific colors on house exteriors. I have already discussed conflicts between Anglos and Portuguese immigrants in Eastern Canada about color use. It is, therefore, significant that changes toward the Anglo norm in Mexican-American housescapes depend on the length of residence in the U.S. (i.e., on acculturation). (I have already discussed this process among Mexican immigrants regarding space use within dwellings.) Another conflict described by *The New York Times* in 1987 concerned self-built houses of Laotians in a rural area of the U.S. Locals complained that it made the neighborhood look like a "Southeast Asian village" and that it should be replaced by something "American." Built environments clearly do communicate identity. But so do other things.

Certain groups use a variety of elements, such as clothing, beards and hairstyles, language, behavior, and various specialized settings and institutions, as well as non-visual components of ambience. The general importance of identity (i.e., of 'culture') means that almost any element can be invested with meaning and used to establish and maintain identity. Even food can be used for that purpose. For example, the different Indian tribes in the Amazon Rainforest have different diets, even though the same foods are available to all. Eating (or not eating) certain classes of animals becomes a badge of particular groups; it is used by them to set themselves apart, i.e., to mark cultural boundaries. This is used by anthropologists to identify various tribes (as are body and facial decorations and material culture, including houses). Even in the U.S. during Thanksgiving dinner (an *American* holiday), different ethnic groups eat very different foods to maintain their identity.

Although a wide variety of means are used to establish and maintain identity, dwellings and other built environments often play a very important role. A student of mine, Paul Maas, analyzing housing advertisements in Chicago newspapers, titled his term paper "You are where you live." The discussion of diet in the Amazon area was titled "You are what you eat."[61]

It has also been pointed out that the complaints about the lack of identity in suburbia are mistaken. In fact, "identity actually flourishes" in Phoenix subdivisions.[62] Identity varies with location, age of developments, the various population groups involved, and specific names of the developments. Other cues are also used and personalization, common in all developments, is more common in lower-priced areas whereas institutionalized elements are more common in higher-priced subdivisions. The same relation was found by a student of mine, Wes Janz, in Milwaukee between lower status areas on the South Side that had higher degrees of personalization than did higher status areas like the East Side.

That built environments and identity are related is clear from attempts (usually unsuccessful) in a number of developing countries to retain, or create, identity through buildings. I have already suggested earlier that this may not be appropriate for certain building types. Little serious research has been done on this topic and needs to be done. Results may then be more successful. In addition to buildings, there may be possibilities in the use of fixed and semi-fixed elements at various other scales: landscape, settlement, and neighborhood. This is a topic that should interest readers of this book.

Many more examples could be given, and even more identified, through a more systematic and formal literature search. But the important points have, I believe, been made. The first is that 'culture' is a most important aspect of environment-behavior relations and cannot be neglected. The second is that whereas 'culture,' as such, does not help much in understanding or designing built environments (and I have used housing as an example), once dismantled, the specific, more concrete expressions of culture are easily used. The approach also makes possible the use of material from, and the ability to relate a large number of fields, other than EBS, and it allows the use of a wide range of evidence, including the popular media.

Scientific 'holism'

It will also have been noted that, as was to have been expected, cross-referencing among the variables was necessary; although I did not emphasize this synthesis, it is an essential next step. Although the whole forms a system, it can only be studied through analysis, and then synthesis, at a higher level. Whereas 'holism' is impossible, hence the need for dismantling, scientific holism is essential and requires three steps, which one can propose as an agenda. First, all the variables identified need to be studied and new ones, if any, discovered. Second, the relative contribution of the variables, their ranking or importance, needs to be established, both in general and for any given case or situation. This will also clarify the interplay of constancy and change, uniformity and generality (or specificity). Third, these variables then need to be reassembled, or synthesized, and their interrelationships and linkages established.

Postscript — the need for open-ended design

'Loose fit' vs. 'tight fit'

There is one point which, although not directly part of the discussion about the role of culture in design, needs to be made, albeit briefly. In my discussion I have emphasized the intimate link between culture and built form and the importance of congruence between the two for purposes of creating supportive environments. This might suggest that the goal, or objective, of design should be 'tight fit,' that environments should be 'tailored' very specifically for given groups. While it is essential that environments be culture-specific, the relationship between culture and built form should be one of 'loose fit,' that design be as open-ended as possible. The question then becomes why that should be and what that might mean. This cannot be discussed here in detail, but a brief discussion is essential.

In this book I have emphasized not only the large number of user groups and the differences among them but also the fact that culture and its expressions and components change, that they are dynamic. Furthermore, it is clear that the rate of culture-change is rapid and seems to be accelerating due to modernization, ethnic revivals, globalization, fads and fashions, the greater role of wants (as opposed to needs), and technological change. Travel and migrations are also increasing rapidly, leading to various forms of acculturation and syncretism, with consequent rapid changes in all the expressions of culture discussed. There is also what is called 'ecological succession' in cities — the nature of populations in various neighborhoods and buildings change over time with changing needs; there is also the decline and revival (e.g., gentrification) of areas. This means that it is undesirable and unadvisable to have too tight a fit between culture and environment. As a result, housing, other building types, and settlements need to have a loose fit (i.e., be flexible and adaptable) to remain supportive despite all these changes. Economics and sustainability also require that environments be able to respond to changes over time, over the whole life of the environments in question.

As just one example, a student of mine, Sean O'Donnell, in a Master's thesis, studied the many changes that occurred in a few blocks of Manhattan between first settlement in the 17th century and 1995. As a result of these, and a more detailed study of current changes in that area as "Little Italy" was being replaced by Chinatown, it became possible to identify some of the physical and regulatory urban frameworks that would make such changes easier.

These various terms — loose fit, flexibility, adaptability, and responsiveness — are subsumed by the term open-endedness, the product being *open-ended design*.[63] In principle, the question should be what is the least possible that can validly and usefully be designed, rather than the maximum, which precludes all change. The need is to think in terms of building and urban frameworks within which users can manipulate the infill. Such frameworks are not only physical but also regulatory and in terms of public (as opposed to private) responsibility and when in the process they occur. These will not be the same in each case. What varies, how much it varies, who makes the changes, when and how often will vary. So will the frameworks — their

Open-ended design

125

nature and who is responsible for them. The process and approach are the same, the products will vary.

In this case also, developing countries provide a useful 'model system.' The many spontaneous settlements, their continual upgrading, rural to urban migration, and hence acculturation, rapidly changing values, ideals, lifestyles, social structures, and other aspects of culture result in dramatic examples of transformations of environments.[64] There is also a very large literature on them. It thus becomes a useful starting point for the study of open-endedness.

For the purposes of this book, the important point is that the typical architect's desire to over-design needs to be replaced by efforts to under-design, to discover the extent to which one can do so. This needs to be combined with a change from designing for one's own culture to understanding and designing for users' cultures and basing design on research in EBS, anthropology, and the other relevant fields (discussed at the beginning). Such changes should transform architecture and design so that it, in fact, does what it claims to do and is supposed to do — create better (i.e., more supportive) environments.

FOOTNOTES

1. It might even be suggested that blocked or greatly restricted choice is a major environmental problem, but this is a different (although important) topic.

2. This is not the place to deal with the question of theory development, although I have discussed it in several publications, most recently Rapoport A (2000) Science, explanatory theory and environment-behavior studies. In S Wapner, *et al.* (Eds.), *Theoretical perspectives in environment-behavior research.* New York: Kluwer Academic/Plenum Publishers, pp. 107-140.

3. Rapoport A (1992) On cultural landscapes. *Traditional Dwellings and Settlements Review* 3(2):33-47; Rapoport A (1990) *History and precedent in environmental design.* New York: Plenum.

4. The more general, extremely important question is: Who does what, where, when, including/excluding whom, and why?

5. Density and crowding are themselves culturally relative, so that 'high density' in the U.S., Spain, and Hong Kong clearly mean very different things. Also, dwellings seen as overcrowded in one culture may not be so evaluated in another. This has major effects on preference and choice, as we will see later.

6. It should also be emphasized that the concept of 'space' is rather more complex than is usually thought. There are many 'kinds' (or 'types') of space and one needs to be specific about which is meant.

7. This is developed in the Epilogue to the 1990 edition of my book, *The Meaning of the Built Environment,* Tucson: University of Arizona Press. Briefly, it is the idea that cues elicit a "frame," e.g., a restaurant. The frame, in turn, elicits a "script," a repertoire of appropriate actions, their sequence, etc. Note also that culture plays a role — unless restaurants are known, the frame doesn't appear and there is no script. Also, the specific actions, their sequence, etc. may vary in different cultures.

8. This is proposed in Moore GT, Tuttle DP, Howell SC (1985) *Environmental design research directions.* New York: Praeger.

9. In this case, (Zeisel J (1973) Symbolic meaning of space and the physical dimension of social relations. In J Walton and DE Carns (Eds.),

Cities in change: Studies on the urban condition. Boston: Allyn and Bacon, pp. 252-263) virtually every aspect of the dwelling had to be redesigned because of latent aspects of activities: entrance, living room and its location, relation of rooms to the street through windows (because of particular uses of windows), and so on.

10. Available data made it impossible to identify differences among smaller groups in those countries.

11. This concept was developed by Stephen and Rachel Kaplan, University of Michigan, and their collaborators.

12. It raises a most important question about the nature of design, although that is a different topic I have discussed elsewhere. For the most recent discussion, see Rapoport A (1995) On the nature of design. *Practices* 3(4):32-43.

13. The general method of dismantling discussed earlier is applicable here as well. A first list of the components of ambience can be found in Rapoport A (1992) On regions and regionalism. In NC Markovich, *et al.* (Eds.), *Pueblo style and regional architecture.* New York: Van Nostrand-Reinhold (paperback), pp. 272-294, esp. pp. 276-280.

14. Other terms used and found in the literature are "unpack" and "unbundle." Note that implicitly, and in a rather weak form, this is already present in Rapoport A (1969) *House form and culture.* Englewood Cliffs, NJ: Prentice-Hall, where I use religion, basic needs, family, position of women, privacy, and social intercourse as ways of trying to link housing and culture.

15. See Barnett R (1977) The libertarian suburb: Deliberate disorder. *Landscape* 22:44-48.

16. See Rapoport A (1992) On regions and regionalism. In NC Markovich, *et al.* (Eds.), *Pueblo style and regional architecture.* New York: Van Nostrand-Reinhold (paperback), pp. 272-294, esp. pp. 276-280.

17. Bishop J (1984) Passing in the night: Public and professional views of Milton Keynes. *Places* 1(4):9-16.

18. Hunt Thompson Associates (1988) *Maiden Lane: Feasibility study* (January). London: Hunt Thompson Associates.

19. Nasar JL, Kang J (1989) A post-jury evaluation: The Ohio State University competition for a center for the visual arts. *Environment and Behavior* 21(4):464-484.

Footnotes

20. See Rapoport A (1990) *The meaning of the built environment*. Tucson: University of Arizona Press (Revised Edition).

21. See Rapoport A (1969) The Pueblo and the Hogan: A cross-cultural comparison of two responses to an environment. In P Oliver (Ed.), *Shelter and society*. London: Barrie and Rockliffe, pp. 66-79.

22. See Rapoport A (1969) *House form and culture*. Engelwood Cliffs, NJ: Prentice-Hall, Ch. 1.

23. See Rapoport A (1983) Development, culture change, and supportive design. *Habitat International* 7(5/6):249-268; Rapoport A (1988) Spontaneous settlements as vernacular design. In CV Patton (Ed.), *Spontaneous shelter*. Philadelphia: Temple University Press, pp. 51-77; Rapoport A (1994) *Sustainability, meaning and traditional environments*. Berkeley, CA: IASTE/Center of Environmental Design Research, Traditional Dwellings and Settlements Working Paper Series, 75/IASTE 75-94(75).

24. See Hakim BS (1986) *Arabic-Islamic cities: Building and planning principles*. London: KPI; Hakim BS (1994) The "Urf" and its role in diversifying the architecture of traditional Islamic cities. *Journal of Architectural and Planning Research* 11(2):108-127.

25. E.g., Akbar J (1988) *Crisis in the built environment (The case of the Muslim city)*. Singapore: Mimar Books; Rapoport A (1992) On regions and regionalism. In NC Markovich, *et al.* (Eds.), *Pueblo style and regional architects*. New York: Van Nostrand-Reinhold (paperback), pp. 272-294, and references therein to Essex County Council (1973), Ostorwetsky and Bordreuil (1980), Vernez Moudon (1986), and Williams, *et al.* (1987).

26. See Sadalla EK, *et al.* (1977) House form and culture revisited. In P Suedfeld and JA Russell (Eds.), *The behavioral basis of design* (EDRA 7). Stroudsburg, PA: Dowden, Hutchinson and Ross, Bk. 2, pp. 279-284.

27. For more examples and more detail, see Rapoport A (1995 (1980)) Culture, site-layout and housing. In A Rapoport (Ed.), *Thirty-three papers in environment-behavior research*. Newcastle, U.K.: Urban International Press, pp. 313-324.

28. This term is from Siegel BJ (1970) Defensive structuring and environmental stress. *American Journal of Sociology* 76:11-46.

29. 'Suburb' can be defined in several ways: by location, politically, in terms of the characteristics of the population, and in terms of a set of specific attributes of the cultural landscape. I am using only the last of these in this discussion.

30. See Rapoport A (1998) Using "culture" in housing design. *Housing and Society* 25(1/2):1-20, esp. p. 15.

31. See Baumgartner MP (1988) *The moral order of the suburb.* New York: Oxford University Press.

32. See Rapoport A (1983) Development, culture change and supportive design. *Habitat International* 7(5/6):249-268.

33. These are 'internal' reasons. I ignore 'external' reasons, such as ideology, politics, economics, and the like.

34. Kroeber AL, Kluckhohn C (1952) *Culture: A critical review of concepts and definitions.* New York: Vintage Books.

35. See Rapoport A (1977) *Human aspects of urban form.* Oxford: Pergamon Press, esp. pp. 289-298; Altman I (1975) *The environment and social behavior.* Monterey, CA: Brooks/Cole, Ch. 2 and 3.

36. See Rapoport A (1977) *Human aspects of urban form.* Oxford: Pergamon Press, pp. 333-345.

37. All the figures given in this chapter are based on published information. Citing those sources would require too many footnotes. Most of these references can be found in Rapoport A (2000) Theory, culture and housing. *Housing, Theory and Society* 17(4):145-165.

38. Other studies do seem to show regional and socio-economic differences. Again, research is needed.

39. It is important to emphasize the usefulness of analyzing newspapers, magazines, advertising, films, TV, novels, popular music, and the like in EBS research, generally, and regarding culture, specifically.

40. The inability to cluster in such a way was also a problem in London in the 1950s among a working class population in the East End.

41. Studies in South Korea have shown a similar phenomenon — living rooms in apartments are used in ways resembling the use of courtyards in traditional Korean houses.

Footnotes

42. In research among the Tswana in Africa, Graeme Hardie and I found a similar culture-specific use of bedrooms. Major differences regarding kitchens, bathrooms, and dining rooms have also been documented in Kenya. The very different use of space and rooms and different norms of "crowding" have proved to present major problems with house designs for Australian Aborigines that ignore cultural specifics.

43. For references on all these topics, see Rapoport A (2000) Theory, culture and housing. *Housing, Theory and Society* 17(4):145-165.

44. I have discussed these in a number of publications. The dismantling of environmental quality and activities are discussed in this book.

45. I should point out that not everyone accepts this approach. For an explicit rejection by two anthropologists, see Cooper M, Rodman M (1995) Culture and spatial boundaries: Cooperative and non-profit housing in Canada. *Architecture and Behavior* 11(2):123-138, esp. p. 124.

46. See Rapoport A (1990) *The meaning of the built environment.* Tucson: University of Arizona Press (Revised Edition).

47. In the U.S. currently, education is the best overall predictor of lifestyle.

48. Note that in *House Form and Culture,* that concept was already being used, although in a different guise — *Genre de Vie* from French cultural geography.

49. For example, Kenneth Boulding (in (1956) *The Image*, Ann Arbor: University of Michigan Press) proposes 10 aspects of 'image,' which I then combine with other proposals and classify in various ways. See Rapoport A (1977) *Human aspects of urban form.* Oxford: Pergamon Press, pp. 42-47.

50. All my examples in (2000) Theory, culture and housing. *Housing, Theory and Society* 17(4):145-165 are from such media, not including popular music. At a recent conference on culture and environment (*Traditional Environments in a New Millennium*, Amasya, Turkey, 20-23 June 2001), Fahriye Sancar analyzed 80 popular songs over historical time. She showed that one could thus identify people's affective relationships with Istanbul and begin to identify the specific feelings and aspects of the city involved.

51. Available in the U.S. for some time, they are now also becoming available for Western Europe.

52. For more details and references of all of the variables being discussed in Chapter 8, see Rapoport A (2000) Theory, culture and housing. *Housing, Theory and Society* 17(4):145-165.

53. See Rapoport A (1985) Thinking about home environments. In I Altman and CM Werner (Eds.), *Home environments* (Vol. 8 of *Human behavior and environment*). New York: Plenum, pp. 255-286; Rapoport A (1995 (1985)) On diversity: Designing for diversity. In A Rapoport (Ed.), *Thirty-three papers in environment-behavior research*. Newcastle, U.K.: Urban International Press, pp. 373-398; Rapoport A (1990) *The meaning of the built environment*. Tucson: University of Arizona Press (Revised Edition).

54. See Rapoport A (1995 (1990)) Indirect approaches to environment-behavior research. In A Rapoport (Ed.), *Thirty-three papers in environment-behavior research*. Newcastle, U.K.: Urban International Press, pp. 489-512.

55. See Franklin B (2000) Creating supportive environments: Minority ethnic housing associations in British inner cities. *Open House International* 25(2):42-49; Chua BH (1988) Adjusting religious practices to different house forms in Singapore. *Architecture and Behavior* 4(1):3-25; Cooper M, Rodman M (1995) Culture and spatial boundaries: Cooperative and non-profit housing in Canada. *Architecture and Behavior* 11(2):123-138.

56. This was reported in *The Times* (London) on July 2, 1998.

57. For a more detailed discussion and references, see Rapoport A (1997) The nature and role of neighborhoods. *Urban Design Studies* 3:93-118.

58. See Shokoohy M, Shokoohy NH (Eds.) (1994) *Kirtipur (An urban community in Nepal — Its people, town planning, architecture and arts)*. London: Araxus; Shrestha US, *et al.* (1997) Social effects of land use changes in Kirtipur, Nepal. *Urban Design Studies* 3:51-73.

59. Macdonald R (1971) *The way some people die*. New York: Bantam Books.

60. Aird C (1981) *Some die eloquent*. New York: Bantam Books.

61. See Gibbons A (1992) Rain forest diet: You are what you eat. *Science* 255(5041):163.

Footnotes

62. See Blake KS, Arreola DD (1996) Residential subdivision identity in metropolitan Phoenix. *Landscape Journal* 15(1):23-35; Rapoport A (1999 (1987)) On the cultural responsiveness of architecture. In JM Stein and KF Spreckelmeyer (Eds.), *Classic readings in architecture*. New York: McGraw-Hill, pp. 329-338.

63. For a detailed discussion and references, see Rapoport A (1995 (1990/91)) Flexibility, open-endedness and design. In A Rapoport (Ed.), *Thirty-three papers in environment-behavior research*. Newcastle, U.K.: Urban International Press, pp. 529-562; Rapoport A (1999 (1987)) On the cultural responsiveness of architecture. In JM Stein and KF Spreckelmeyer (Eds.), *Classic readings in architecture*. New York: McGraw-Hill, pp. 329-338.

64. One recent example is Tipple G (2000) *Extending themselves (User-initiated transformations of government-built housing in developing countries)*. Liverpool, U.K.: Liverpool University Press.

INDEX

Index

Amos Rapoport is Distinguished Professor Emeritus in the School of Architecture and Urban Planning at the University of Wisconsin-Milwaukee, where he was previously Professor of Architecture and Anthropology. He received his Bachelor's degree in Architecture from Melbourne University (Australia), his Master's in Architecture from Rice University as a Fulbright student, and his Postgraduate Diploma of Town and Regional Planning from the University of Melbourne. He has taught at the Universities of Melbourne and Sydney (Australia), the University of California at Berkeley, and University College London. He has held visiting appointments in Israel, Turkey, Britain, Argentina, Brazil, Canada, Puerto Rico, India, and Switzerland, among others, and has lectured by invitation all over the world. He is a registered Architect in two states in Australia, a Fellow of the Royal Australian Institute of Architects, and an Associate of the Royal Institute of British Architects.

As one of the founders of the new field of Environment-Behavior Studies, Rapoport's work has mainly focused on the role of cultural variables, cross-cultural studies, and theory development and synthesis. He is the editor or co-editor of four books and several monographs and the author of approximately 200 papers, chapters, and the like, as well as six books (including this one) and several monographs. His work has been translated into a number of languages, including French, Spanish, German, Greek, Japanese, Chinese, and Korean.